Real or Not?

Health Scams and Beauty Fallacies Exposed

REAL OR NOT?

Health Scams and Beauty Fallacies Exposed

Andy Ho, PhD

The Straits Times
Singapore

World Scientific DL Publishing

Published by

DL Publishing, an imprint of
World Scientific Publishing Co. Pte. Ltd.
5 Toh Tuck Link, Singapore 596224
USA office: 27 Warren Street, Suite 401-402, Hackensack, NJ 07601
UK office: 57 Shelton Street, Covent Garden, London WC2H 9HE

Library of Congress Cataloging-in-Publication Data
Ho, Andy, Ph.D.
Real or not : health scams and beauty fallacies exposed / by Andy Ho.
p. cm.
Includes index.
ISBN 981-256-277-X (pbk. : alk. paper)
1. Quacks and quackery. 2. Medical misconceptions. 3. Medical care--Corrupt practices. 4. Cosmetics industry--Corrupt practices. 5. Pharmaceutical industry--Corrupt practices. 6. Deceptive advertising. 7. Fraud. I. Title.

R730.H597 2005
615.8'56--dc22

2005041837

British Library Cataloguing-in-Publication Data
A catalogue record for this book is available from the British Library.

The articles in this book were first published in *The Straits Times* between 2003 and 2004.

Typeset by Stallion Press
Email: enquiries@stallionpress.com

Printed in Singapore by Mainland Press

This volume is dedicated to my wife, Josephine,
my son, Ken, and my daughter, Jean.

Preface

WILL that really make my breasts larger? Can lasers actually make my skin younger? Which is better for me, Viagra or Cialis? What do you mean my liver enzymes are high, Doctor? Should I drink red wine to keep my ticker healthy? Should I take that neurolinguistic programming class to improve my performance at work? How low should be my cholesterol?

If you or your significant other — wife/husband, girlfriend/boyfriend — has ever asked these questions and others, I think you will appreciate a well-researched answer from someone other than your doctor who may, anyway, be too busy with his daily grind to keep up with any literature. It was with this in mind that I began writing a Saturday column called "Science Monitor" for *The Straits Times,* Singapore's main daily, focussing on various health scams, fantasies and fallacies that have begun plaguing consumers in Asia. They were always crafted in response to new medical developments reported in the media or triggered off by interesting questions posed by my readers who often call in or e-mail me.

This book is a compilation of some of my more recent columns. I have grouped 40 of them into five chapters. In addition, I have written an essay especially for this book, one on anal sex, a matter one prudish night editor at *The Straits Times* considered too scatological to publish in a family newspaper — as if families did not originate from sex in the broadest sense.

But I think it is an important issue to address which the mainstream press, whether in Asia or even in the West, has become too politically correct when it comes to gay or HIV issues that it can't address them honestly and truthfully. If you have a gay son or colleague, the facts I lay out in this essay may well save his life.

I wrote the essay precisely because that dishonesty is symptomatic of much in the press which has engendered a not-unjustified decline in trust for journalists, which has only been matched by a similarly growing mistrust of physicians and Western medicine.

Even as the science of medicine advances, the general public's confidence in them has seriously down-trended in recent years. Correlatively, this has given rise to a widespread interes. and unexamined trust in alternative medicine, so-called.

But this means the popularity of much that is really quackery and the unjustified but widespread confidence in herbal concoctions and nutritional supplements have given the unscrupulous scammer many a market opportunity.

Many of us are fools when it comes to these things and, as the old saw goes, a fool and his money are soon parted. In this case, however, the scams foisted on us could harm us, health-wise.

I decided to compile these columns together as a handy little book to provide for you a review of what cutting-edge research says about these scams. You can apply the insights culled from the best studies about health claims of various alternative therapies that I have reviewed painstakingly and discussed with the best scientists and doctors. Rest assured, dubious medical practices that trained health-care professionals including physicians are not spared either.

Above all, I urge readers to do what I have done: Research any claim for your money that says it can make you healthier, happier or hipper, all without the deleterious side effects of your doctor's prescription. Begin your search with a huge dollop of salt in each case and you will soon learn to ferret out the truth for yourself.

Organise the pros and cons.

Then decide for yourself.

But remember also to keep an open mind.

You might be surprised, as I have been, by what you find after a duly diligent search.

But, most of all, trust your own research.

It only remains for me to thank my family for putting up with my spending innumerable hours poring over medical journals or spending time on the phone late into the night talking to physicians and scientists who practise in other time zones and who are always gracious with their time when I call to discuss their research.

Andy Ho, PhD (M.I.T.)
Singapore
2005

Contents

Introduction

IN July 2004, a British surgeon ticked off Prince Charles, the heir to the British throne, for promoting the likes of Gerson Therapy — coffee enemas and carrot juice — for terminal cancer. And quite rightly too. In an open letter to the *British Medical Journal,* Dr Michael Baum, professor emeritus of surgery at University College London, thundered: "Your power and authority rest on an accident of birth. I don't begrudge you that authority, but I do beg you to exercise your power with extreme caution when advising patients with life-threatening diseases to embrace unproven therapies ... With respect, Your Highness, you've got it wrong". Wrong because untested and uncontested.

Of course, no one is contesting that herbs may contain useful compounds. After all, doctors have long used digoxin extracted from foxglove to treat heart failure, quinine from the cinchona bark for malaria, and vincristine from rosy periwinkle for leukaemia, and so on. What must be contested, however, is the unquestioning faith in anything calling itself "herbal".

If you want to be sure the herbal concoction you are taking is, firstly, safe and, secondly, efficacious for your condition, there is only one gold standard: All herbs must be subjected to randomised, double-blind, placebo-controlled trials. Any unorthodox therapy will cease to be "alternative" if it meets these strict evidence-based requirements. But if you can't, please hold your peace.

In such drug trials, some test subjects are given the treatment while others are given a look-alike placebo. Neither researcher nor participant knows who has been given what until the study ends — thus both are blinded. Who is assigned to treatment or placebo is done randomly, perhaps by a coin flip — hence, randomised.

Of course, many advocates of alternative medicine have insisted that this gold standard of drug research isn't quite their cup of tea. For them, tradition, anecdotal evidence and user testimonial should suffice. After all, if a treatment helps me or my grandmother, it must be effective.

If not, it doesn't work.

Simple enough?

Unfortunately, common sense observations like these aren't reliable in medical conditions, and double-blind studies have repeatedly proven this to be the case. This is because observations can be confounded by biases, placebo effects and pure chance.

Without fair tests, we may risk accepting useless or harmful treatments as helpful and safe, or dismissing actually effective treatments as useless. This is all the more true with "traditional" cures, for a few other reasons.

First, it is not every day that drugs produce distinct and dramatic effects like opium for pain or chloroform for anaesthesia. Where there are no such dramatic effects, especially with herbs, more formal comparisons are needed to assess their effects.

Second, herbal cures can be harmful. Some herbs can cause DNA damage but the effects may be seen only in later generations. For example, naturopaths advise arthritis patients to take almonds and sunflower seeds that are very rich in omega-6-polyunsaturated fatty acids. But these can actually aggravate the inflammation.

Third, common sense seems to fly out of the window whenever the phrase complementary/alternative/traditional medicine gets up on its hind legs. It is, quite simply, a very emotive issue. To detractors, it means quackery, pure and simple, never mind that peppermint can alleviate symptoms in irritable bowel syndrome. To supporters, it spells natural, safe and painless, never mind that St John's wort, a herb taken for mild depression, reacts dangerously with warfarin, a blood thinner. If this leads to underdosing of warfarin, a blood clot could occur; if it leads to overdosing of warfarin, serious bleeding could ensue.

To overcome this partisanship, all alternative therapies must be tested fairly. Insisting that even the most ardently believed folk remedy be subjected to the most rigorous of tests isn't being anti-tradition. It is simply doing good science, there being neither Western nor Eastern science, just good or bad science. On a practical note, doctors must face up to the reality that what was once weird and wacky is increasingly seen as acceptable, even cool. Many may be taking alternative medicines but aren't telling their doctors, who aren't bothering to ask.

To the doctor: This is an explosive mix. Physicians must no longer irresponsibly bury their heads in the sand and exclude a whole strain of health care — legitimate or otherwise — as if it has nothing to do with them and their patients. Yes, they didn't learn about such things in medical school but most alternative medications remain untested and unresearched, so they make for potentially dangerous situations. Doctors must support and keep up with the scientific study of herbal medicines.

To the consumer: You owe yourself and your family the duty of finding out as much as you can about alternative therapies that clamour for your time, money and health. To be forewarned is to be forearmed.

I. Shy about sexy matters?

Boob creams and pills are just a bust

WANT bigger breasts? Though breast implants have been around for 40 years, doctors are still unsure about their long-term risks. These days — what with globalisation of Hollywood culture — many women may want a lift. But they fear the scalpel, so they try out the many pills, lotions, creams and devices advertised as breast developers instead.

It's a huge market. But are women letting their insecurity about their bodies get ahead of their reason?

Most of these non-surgical methods are likely to give only flat results.

They may seem quite genuine, what with testimonials from "real people" as well as money-back guarantees, but it is worth remembering that beauty products — unlike prescription drugs — are not regulated and don't need government approval or testing before they are marketed.

Consider the various methods that purport to enlarge breasts. First, exercises. Since the breasts are composed primarily of glands and fat, no amount of exercise will change their actual size or shape.

At best, some devices may help develop the muscles that support the breasts. When these muscles are larger and firmer, they push the breasts outwards, giving the illusion of larger breasts.

What about the various bust-o-lift creams and lotions?

In theory, lotions and creams loaded with the female hormone called estrogen might do the trick by stimulating the growth of the glands in the breast. Applying estrogen cream could increase breast size — as long as it is applied.

But unless the cream is one prescribed by a doctor, it is likely to have so little estrogen you might as well smear salsa on your chest.

Even if you get your hands on an unlimited supply of full-strength estrogen cream, don't be overjoyed: Over-stimulating breast growth with hormones can predispose one to cancer. So a cream or lotion (or pill) that actually works but is not a prescription item is likely to be one chock-full of estrogen, perhaps imported illegally.

But marketers of these creams, lotions and pills do not highlight their estrogen content. Instead, they are generally made out to be herbal in origin — containing harmless "plant estrogens" that are apparently found in some 300 plants like *dong quai*, soybean, oat bran, fenugreek, wild yam, saw palmetto and so on.

Of course, being herbal, they are also touted as natural and safe.

Yet one was recently withdrawn from the market — GroBust. When its makers were first sued in the US, it listed Kava, a South Pacific herb, among its ingredients — before Kava's potential to cause fatty liver became known. This example suggests how there is often no scientific justification for calling such products "safe".

Almost no non-surgical method has been documented to be effective — and documentation is no easy task.

First, proper steps must be taken to ensure that any "before and after" differences don't arise from estrogen intake, observer bias, body weight changes, body fluid content changes with the menstrual cycle or time of day, measuring at different points on different occasions, and postural variations.

Second, the woman should be measured at the same time of day, applying the tape with the same tautness each time while her posture and position should remain the same.

Third, to safeguard against fraud, there should be several independent observers with videotape and/or photographic documentation. To ascertain there is permanent breast enlargement, follow-up checks are needed for years. The breasts should also be scanned with MRI to ensure no disease develops.

Impossible standards?

Before you lose all hope, there is one device that might just pass muster: The computerised vacuum bra that fits over the breasts and must be worn without interruption for ten hours a day for three months.

Developed by a plastic surgeon, it supposedly exploits the principle of tissue expansion used over the last 30 years to grow tissue to lengthen limbs, for instance.

The vacuum supposedly stretches breast tissue gently, and when healthy cells are stretched, they respond by first swelling temporarily, then eventually dividing and replicating to accommodate the stretch force, thus generating new breast tissue.

The results of a tiny trial of 12 women begun in 1998 were published in a mainstream journal, *Plastic & Reconstructive Surgery,* in 2000. There was an average increase of one cup size 15 months after treatment ended. A follow-up study of 30 women by another group replicated these results.

A larger study by the original group involving 95 women has just been completed with similar results and awaits publication if their peers adjudge the study to have scientific merit. All three studies abided with the strict guidelines suggested above.

If it truly works, how many women will stick to it in this hot weather? Its hard, protuberant cones can't be concealed even under the largest sweatshirt you can wear in the office. If you knock into your colleagues or filing cabinets, one of the domes may come unstuck — and with that, a loud giveaway alarm will sound.

There'll be loud guffaws in the office — or you'll be rudely awakened in the middle of the night if you go to sleep with them. By the way, you won't be able to sleep on your belly for the three months you wear them. If you are very lean or you are Asian — which supposedly means tighter skin — you'll get slower breast growth than a fatter woman or a white sister.

Still, if there is growth without the scalpel, many may just grin and bear it.

Do beauty salons have this contraption? No, the gadget is available through doctors in the United States only.

Looks like it's bra-burning time

IN 2004, some lingerie merchants in various parts of the world began a counterintuitive advertising campaign which declared that bras cause breast cancer, so women should stop wearing bras. Which magnificent marketing genius thought this up is not a concern here, neither his rationale. And without impugning the motives of a bra seller telling women not to buy his bras, that claim was largely based on a faulty study, *Dressed To Kill* (1995, Avery Publishing).

In the said book, the authors, husband-and-wife team Syd and Soma Singer, argue that bras with underwires squeeze breasts until they can't drain lymph. A clear fluid that moves through our arteries and tissues, lymph is laden with cancer-causing toxins that we all absorb from the environment, they said. Over time, they argued, these toxins linger to cause breast cancer.

Alas for the Singers, experts have roundly dismissed their cancer theory. It is true that, despite numerous studies since the 18th century, lymphatic physiology of the human body, breasts included, is still not completely understood. Nevertheless, it is fair to say that the research on which *Dressed To Kill* itself was based was manifestly and fatally flawed.

How so?

We do know that arteries carry fresh blood to all parts of the body, breasts included, while used blood leaves the breasts through veins and is pumped back to the lungs to be refreshed.

The arteries also bring lymph, which then leaves the bloodstream to circulate through tissues, cleansing them. Next, fine vessels called lymphatics collect the used lymph to drain it back into the body's central drainage system. Along the lymphatics, there are stations, or nodes, which filter out and trap bugs, cancer cells and toxins.

Think of arteries as two-lane highways bringing oxygen and nutrients to the breasts, and veins as one-lane highways taking used blood away, with lymphatics forming another one-lane highway channelling lymph away.

In short, two similar lanes in, two different lanes out. Whereas the heart pumps blood through the arteries and veins, lymph flows along the lymphatics passively when their surrounding tissues move.

Whence cometh the Singers' ideas about a bra-lymph connection?

Women in poorer countries generally go bra-less, the Singers noted, as they have done for millennia. The couple reasoned that natural breast movements that occur with every step taken give bra-less women a healthy breast lymphatic circulation — until bras immobilise and constrict it. For example, while Australian aboriginal women have virtually no breast cancer — they aren't assimilated into the mainstream white culture — Maori women in New Zealand, who are Westernised bra-wearers, have high breast cancer rates.

To substantiate their postulate, the Singers interviewed some 4,730 American women. They found that women who wore bras for 24 hours daily were 125 times more likely to have breast cancer than those who went bra-less, 113 times more often if they wore the bra for 12 hours each day.

That's a striking discovery — if true. But there are a couple of problems. First, there are no peer-reviewed studies that report a bra-cancer association, or that bras cause toxins to accumulate in the breasts. Second, the Singer study did not exclude other risk factors as good studies should. Their sample was a biased one — all Caucasian, mostly "medium income", aged 30 to 79 — half of whom had had breast cancer. This reason, among others, made it unsuitable for publication in reputable journals.

If you have a startling hypothesis, you need to build up a body of work by first publishing in reputable journals because publication signals that your research is rigorous and credible to your peers. If a consensus forms that you are on the right track, you might then publish a book about it, citing chapter and verse from your own work or the work of others. Instead, the Singers fired off what they called their "explosive" survey findings to the most prestigious cancer research institutes. None responded. The reason, the Singers surmised, was that the lingerie business, like the cancer business, was huge, so vested interests were stacked against them.

Third, a controversial hypothesis must withstand the hazards of refutation.

From 2001, the Singers say, they have been comparing Fijian women, half of whom wear bras and half of whom don't. While both groups live in the same environment and eat the same diet, the bra-wearers get breast cancer at the same rates as US women do, while bra-less Fijian women have almost no breast cancer.

If true, this would be strongly supportive evidence — but it has only been issued as press releases and hasn't been published in any mainstream journal.

The Singers, who have no bona fide academic appointments, solicit — on the Internet — for financial contributions to fund their research, which they conduct from their "institute", a 27 hectare farm in Hawaii.

Their supporters, even if they grant that their research methods aren't up to scratch, could still argue that there is merit to their bra-squeezed lymph argument itself. As the Singers say that "because lymphatic vessels are very thin, they are extremely sensitive to pressure and are easily compressed".

Yes, tight bras with underwires do leave red marks and creases on the skin so they might impede the set of superficial lymphatics that drains lymph from the breast skin and the other set that drains the nipples.

However, the breast has a third and deeper set of lymphatics that drains deep breast tissues. This is the very set involved in the spread of breast cancer and is removed during cancer surgery. But it is too deep for bras to impinge on, so its lymph should move around as the breasts move inside a bra.

Yes, there is even at least one study (published in the *European Journal of Cancer* in 1991 entitled "Breast size, handedness and breast cancer risk" by CC Hsieh and D Trichopoulos) which found that "women who do not wear bras had half the risk of breast cancer compared with bra users (but) possibly because they are thinner and likely to have smaller breasts, (which) may be a risk factor for breast cancer".

Nevertheless, the advice to stop wearing bras does make sense.

First, wearing a bra may make the breasts warmer and it is known that hotter surface areas of the breast are associated with cancer. The temperature of the breast can be measured using thermography, where heat sensitive cameras show that bra-free breasts are cooler while areas at the lower edges of a bra where there is pressure on the skin and areas covered by seams where the material has more than one thickness are warmer.

It is known that the pre-cancerous breast — the breast that's going to get cancer in women who are predisposed to breast cancer — is a half a degree centigrade warmer than the normal breast. So anything like the bra that raises the temperature of the breasts should raise some eyebrows.

That is, bras may theoretically have an effect, perhaps a very small effect, but it is difficult to give women definite advice unless there is better data, which should come in the years ahead as Hugh Simpson, a Scottish cancer specialist at the Glasgow Royal Infirmary has developed the ChronoBra, which measures breast temperature changes during the menstrual cycle.

Second, published research also suggests that the pressure exerted by conventional bras especially at the sides also impact the autonomous nervous system — the part that is not under our voluntary control which regulates heart rate, blood pressure, even gut activity, cor or internal body temperature, and so on.

Third, it is a myth foisted on women that bras keep the breasts perky. Bras are marketed as being essential for support but there is no evidence that wearing a bra could prevent sagging, because the breast itself is not muscle, so keeping it toned up is impossible.

All — except fairly tiny breasts — must eventually sag with age as milk glands get replaced by fat and gravity does its work on the breasts' Cooper's ligaments, delicate supportive tissues that hold up the glandular tissues of the breast.

That is, breast tissue contains no muscle, only glands, lymphatics, fat and these ligaments which, once stretched, never return to their original position.

In fact, women didn't always wear bras.

Introduced 80 years ago, the rationale for wearing a bra has changed over the decades. First they covered up, next they lifted and supported, finally, they enlarge and reveal women's breasts. Bras are marketed on sex appeal. So, if a woman wants a particular contour for her chest under her clothes, she will buy a particular brand, and that is what they're designed for.

That is, bras have no permanent effect on the shape of your breasts. A bra gives you the shape it's designed to give while you wear it. Take it off and you are *au naturel*.

When one looks for positive evidence that bras are good for health, it does not exist. So here's the skinny on bras: Except as a habit, there's just no good reason to wear a bra. If modesty is a concern, loose camisoles will do fine.

One exception, though.

When a woman frequently engages in high impact activities like aerobics, jogging or horse back riding, there is a lot of bouncing which puts extra stress on the Cooper's ligaments. Bounce or vertical movements of the breasts can stretch the Cooper's ligaments irreversibly.

After all, vigorous exercising may cause up to 40 kg of impact on the breasts. Here's where the extra support a sports bra can give comes in. Created in the 1970s by two female marathoners who developed some breast problems — pain from chafing, bleeding nipples, etc — from running long distances, the first sports bra was really just two jock straps for men sewn together. Later, it went into commercial production as the Jogbra, that promised to prevent undue movement of the breasts during exercise.

Today's sports bras are better made from better material that keeps moisture away from the skin and allows sweat to evaporate quickly while controlling chafing. The best ones have no metal or plastic parts or underwires and provide excellent support from both the cup area and shoulder straps, cradling the breasts close to the body and offering full support with minimal bounce.

Their shoulder straps are non-stretching and are wide enough to prevent abrasive injury while distributing weight evenly over your shoulders. Good sports bras also have no seams across any potentially moving areas. (Seams can abrade or blister.) Some also have extended midriff sections to stop the bra riding up during vigorous activity.

It takes a lot of shopping around to find the right sports bra for your figure and breast size — but it is time well spent because the wrong sports bra can restrict movement, cause chafing and irritation, shoulder and back pain, restrict sweat evaporation, and worst of all, provide inadequate support to reduce bounce.

You wouldn't want that to happen.

In search of manhood boost? Here're some phallic fallacies

GUYS, do you remember being that eight-year-old trying a far arc while urinating, then boasting you hit farther than anyone else? Male preoccupation with the penis starts very young and not infrequently becomes a hankering for a larger one as boys grow up.

This has been true across time and cultures. The Kamasutra lionises the well-endowed Ushvah, or Stallion Man. Ancient Romans worshipped a deity named Priapus, whose name is immortalised in the word "priapism", or painful erections that refuse to subside for hours.

Still, penis size isn't something men talk about unabashedly. A certain furtiveness pervades any such discussion. This may explain the success of Internet spammers who flood e-mail in-boxes with promises to boost your manhood, money-back guaranteed.

But men with low self-esteem are hardly the only ones taken in. In August 2003, for example, a security flaw at the "Amazing Internet Products" website left an order log exposed, revealing the identities of 6,000 people who had actually ordered the company's Pinnacle herbal pills at US$50 a bottle. These people weren't exactly failures in life: According to a wired.com investigation, they included the manager of a US$6 billion mutual fund, the president of an airplane parts company, the head of a credit-repair firm, and so on.

Perhaps these products do work then?

Alas, they don't. There is absolutely no evidence in any peer-reviewed journal — one where the logic and rigour of one's research is checked by independent experts — that any non-surgical method can produce a permanent increase in adult penis size.

Yes, applying testosterone cream can increase penis size in adolescents who are running low on the male hormone. But there is no proof any unguent, including testosterone cream, can soup up the adult organ.

No pill, herbal or otherwise, can affect the size permanently, just as there are no pills that can specifically enlarge your nose or biceps. Neither will Viagra. That pill helps with impotence, not size.

What about weight training then?

Proponents claim that men of the Sadhu tribe of the upper Ganges hang weights from their penises to lengthen them. They reason that any tissue can be stretched permanently: Just look at the long-necked women of the Padaung tribe in northern Thailand who wear heavy brass ornaments around their necks.

Worn from the age of six, with more added each year, these heavy coils end up deforming the collar bone and upper ribs, pushing them down so they appear to be part of a long neck. It's all a cruel optical illusion.

The phallus' construction, however, makes such an illusion well nigh impossible. The organ is made up of three cylindrical bodies of spongy tissue that fill with blood to produce an erection. The trio are surrounded by a semi-elastic white sheath, which may be likened to a bicycle tyre that stops the inner tube from expanding forever. In the same way, the sheath's stretch limits define the erect penis size.

A vacuum device may produce a small, temporary increase in size as long as the pump is in use. Penile tissue is elastic, so it stretches like a rubber band. But remove the device and the penis snaps right back to its original size.

Perhaps weights could stretch the sheath permanently? There is no research to confirm or disprove this, but accidents with such weight exercises have been known to result in serious tears to the sheath. More often, these weight and stretching exercises are premised on the penis being like the biceps or other skeletal muscles which can be buffed up. However, the only muscles found in the penis are smooth muscles in the walls of the arteries that feed blood into the three chambers, producing erections. Unlike the biceps, smooth muscles there or anywhere in the body cannot be toned up with exercise.

True, six weeks after some penile surgery, doctors have their patients attach a small vacuum cup to the penile head, so that a weight can be hung on the metal hook at the bottom of the cup for an hour or so every day for months. A weight sleeve that looks like a heavy sock can also be worn on the penis all day long.

But these are devices used to prevent scars from forming after surgery to straighten crooked members. The object is to avoid serious scarring that would deform the penis again.

That surgery, incidentally, is also different from the dangerous, experimental lengthening procedure, where the ligament anchoring the penis to the pelvic bone is snipped. The portion of the penis that is normally lurking inside the body, like roots under a tree trunk, is thus cut loose to fall forward and hang out, giving the illusion of an added inch. That ligament, however, keeps the erect penis pointing upwards. Cut loose from its moorings, the erect member points down towards the floor instead. It becomes unstable, and slips and jars during sex. Held up, it sinks down into the scrotum, looking like a long-nosed hound with big floppy ears.

Any foray into penile enlargement territory, surgical or non-surgical, is thus dicey and unnecessary.

Just be thankful for what you have.

Sexual blues in three colours

MENTION erections and Viagra comes to mind.

For the last five years, that blue, diamond-shaped drug was the only real panacea for men with erectile problems.

With more than one billion pills sold since 1998, and worldwide sales of US$1.7 billion in 2003, it has been a hard act to follow. But two new drugs are now offering it serious competition.

First, there was Cialis (whose chemical name is tadalafil), a yellow tablet and then there was Levitra (vardenafil), a round, orange-coated pill, both hitting the market in several countries in 2003.

All three love potions differ as to when each starts to work, how long the desirable effect lasts, and what the side effects might be. Levitra promises to act faster while Cialis claims to last longer than Viagra (sildenafil). Otherwise, the trio work in the same way on the same processes leading up to an erection, which a wag has likened to how an automatic washing machine works.

When the switch is turned on (the brain fires up), the machine's electric wires (the nerves) carry signals to the inlet (arteries in the penis), which opens up to allow water (blood) in, while shutting off the drain (veins in the penis).

When water has filled up the drum (blood fills up the penis, which stiffens up), the washing cycle begins (sexual intercourse proceeds). At the end of the final wash cycle, the process goes into reverse. The switch shuts off (brain stimuli ends), the inlet closes up (little or no more blood flows into the arteries), the drain opens up (blood flows out of the veins) and the drum empties (the erection subsides).

There is then a spin cycle to wring the clothes dry before the machine can be used for another load. (That's like the period of rest before another erection can be mounted.)

If your wires and the plumbing are working fine, the three drugs won't magnify your erection — or pleasure. After all, putting more water into a filled washing machine won't make the clothes cleaner.

The specific signal that gets it all fired up is a chemical called nitric oxide (NO) that is released in the penis when a man is sexually aroused.

NO eventually produces a certain phosphate which relaxes the arteries in the penis so they fill up with blood.

All three drugs block an enzyme that breaks down the phosphate. This makes sure there is enough phosphate around to do its magic.

The bottom line: No NO, no go.

This fact was discovered in the early 1990s when Pfizer was testing a drug on men with chest pains. Though the drug, called sildenafil, didn't help the pains, patients refused to give it up.

Curious doctors soon found out why: Their heart patients had better erections. Viagra was thus born, offering men the option for the first time in history to pop a pill and have an erection.

The pre-Viagra era now seems like the Dark Ages. Impotent men had to resort to injecting a drug into the penis, inserting a pellet into it, or using mechanical devices like vacuum pumps. If all else failed, there were always surgically-implanted hydraulic pumps.

No wonder men were embarrassed to come forward when the problem raised its ugly head, usually in their fifties and beyond.

Many were also told it was probably all in the mind. Today, doctors say that 80 per cent of impotence cases have underlying physical causes. But while Viagra quickly solved many of these problems, the drug has not been problem-free. There were early reports of heart attacks, which were later shown to be unrelated to Viagra.

Today, the blue bomber carries an alert only for people on certain high blood pressure drugs and nitrites for chest pain. For the rest, it has been like a second birth. Some users say it makes a good thing better!

One weird effect of the blue pill, however, is that it can actually give one's vision a bluish hue. Levitra claims to have less of the blue vision, and there have been no reports of similar phenomena with Cialis.

The new kids on the block also claim faster reaction times and sometimes longer windows of opportunity.

If Viagra takes 60 minutes to work and lasts for four to six hours, Levitra takes 15 minutes to work, and lasts just as long.

Cialis, on the other hand, takes 30 minutes to act but lasts for 24 to 36 hours, so a second sexual encounter is possible. It allows men to choose their intimate moments.

Because sex is not tied to a stopwatch and no one likes it timed to a pill, Cialis quickly grabbed market share after its launch in most places. For example, it captured 25 per cent of the European market — the French call it "the weekender" — and nearly half the market in Singapore.

While all three drugs help men who are only inconsistently able or totally unable to mount an erection, they don't make normal anatomical functions better.

After all, if a washing machine washes clean, you can't get any cleaner. The trio also don't trigger off automatic erections or create arousal where there is none.

All three really help only physical function, not intimacy or emotional relationships.

Men with normal erections should not use them recreationally. It won't help the sex life. Instead, they should pay attention to their relationships, especially in the communication. Those with erectile problems should also do the same while reaching out for these safe and effective drugs. You might see blue for some time, but you won't be singing the blues.

Bye to hormones and back to herbs for hot flushes?

THIS must be a trying time for menopausal women. The hormones prescribed to help them tide over that difficult period are now believed to do more harm than good.

A landmark American study that came out in August 2003 showed that these pills, containing female hormones oestrogen and progesterone, make women more likely to have breast cancer, heart attacks, blood clots, strokes and dementia.

Introduced 60 years ago, its use took off in the 1980s when it came to be seen as the fountain of youth. Perhaps this was why actresses like Elizabeth Taylor continued to look like stunners well into their 50s and 60s.

Menopause occurs when a woman has her last period — when her ovaries stop releasing eggs. On average, this happens around the age of 50 when she passes from the reproductive to the non-reproductive years of her life.

Usually, this is a gradual process but as menopause approaches, the production of hormones by the ovaries slows down and may become erratic.

As a result, menstrual periods become irregular, sometimes bunching much closer together, sometimes getting much further apart.

These fluctuations in a woman's hormones lead to bodily changes, just as they did during her adolescence, only these changes may be more intense now.

Most bothersome of all, there are hot flushes. The woman experiences sudden waves of heat in the upper body that begin with a tingling sensation in the fingers or rapid heart beats.

Next, the skin temperature rises rapidly, sometimes even causing redness in the face. She sweats profusely in the process.

These flushes can last from half to five minutes and if they happen during sleep, drenching sweat can soak the bedding.

However, they tend to be very uncommon five years after menopause.

Such women may also have achy joints, urinate too frequently and have a dry vagina. They could become moody, concentrate or recall less well than before, and may complain of headaches a lot.

These are very real problems that in 10 to 15 per cent of cases need medical attention. But still, they are a temporary phase.

The mood changes and hot flushes may last two or three years, while vaginal dryness and changes in sexual desire may persist after menopause.

As they age, all women do face higher risks of heart disease and osteoporosis (or thinning and weakening of bones with age until they fracture too easily) after menopause.

In fact, it was largely in a bid to stem these problems that doctors first prescribed hormones to replace those that the ovaries no longer produce enough of.

Over the years, even when studies showed a heightened risk of breast cancer, doctors continued to reassure their patients that hormone replacement therapy (HRT), as it was called, promised significant benefits.

These included, they said, protection from heart attacks, osteoporosis, stroke and dementia.

Until August 2003 when a long-running study called the Women's Health Initiative published its final findings in the prestigious *New England Journal of Medicine*.

It read like a litany of horrors.

In women receiving HRT drugs, the incidence of heart attacks rose by 29 per cent, breast cancer by 26 per cent, stroke by 41 per cent, blood clots by 111 per cent, and dementia by 105 per cent.

To be sure, there was a 37 per cent decrease in colon cancer and 33 per cent drop in hip fractures. They were only marginally better when it came to hot flushes, sleep and physical functioning.

These findings were no fluke. They were replicated in a British effort, The Million Women Study, published in an equally prestigious journal, *The Lancet,* at the same time.

Many women stopped HRT therapy when the United States released preliminary results last year. But many also resumed it later as they became miserable without the drug.

Others have turned to "natural phytoestrogens", or oestrogen-like substances from plants such as legumes and cereals, including soy. Anecdotally, Asian women who consume a lot of soy products seem to have less traumatic menopauses.

No one knows for sure whether the traditional Chinese herb, *dong kuai,* or its Western counterpart, black cohosh, works.

Still, the American College of Obstetricians and Gynaecologists has expressed a consensus opinion that black cohosh might help women with hot flushes.

This is a stout, blackish rhizome (or an underground stem like ginger) derived from a species of buttercup that has been used for menopausal problems in the West for centuries.

A black cohosh extract, marketed by GlaxoSmithKline as Remifemin, is still undergoing trials in the US. Some gynaecologists suggest that women should still consider HRT at the lowest dose and for the shortest time, if they really need it. But no one knows what risks this may pose. HRT is a therapy that can be stopped any time and restarted any time. But if a woman has a family history of heart attacks, stroke or cancer, the latest study results should give pause for thought.

Prostates and a sea of pain

THE prostate is a gland found only in the male. Sitting just in front of the rectum and just below the bladder, it produces fluid for semen. The gland wraps around a tube called the urethra, the passage that allows urine to flow from the bladder and out through the penis.

In 80 per cent of men, the prostate gets bigger with age and constricts the urethra, thus causing urine flow to be weaker or slower.

If the gland turns cancerous, its cells produce huge quantities of a protein called the prostate specific antigen (PSA) to fight the tumour.

Before PSA was identified, the main blood test looked for an enzyme produced by cancerous prostate cells — prostatic acid phosphatase (PAP). The male equivalent of the female pap smear to check for cervical cancer, PAP was widely used until 1986, when doctors began telling patients that PSA was better.

However, a Harvard study of 6,691 males published in *The New England Journal of Medicine* in August 2003 says that PSA screening misses most prostate cancers.

Males do not habitually speak of their prostate problems openly. They usually mention it in hushed tones, the way women used to talk about breast cancer.

After all, the treatment of prostate cancer, including radiation and surgery, may lead to incontinence and impotence.

Moreover, confirming prostate cancer involves a painful half-hour procedure, where several biopsy needles are inserted into the area between the anus and the scrotum to get tissue samples.

Prior to this, doctors perform a digital rectal examination, inserting a (gloved) finger into the rectum to feel the prostate. But the entire gland cannot be checked for lumps this way, which is why a PSA test is also done.

Should there be more than four nanograms (or four billionths of a gram) of PSA in each cubic centimeter of blood, the physician will suggest one or more uncomfortable biopsies.

It had been widely assumed that PSA, one of the few cancer-screening tests available, saves lives.

After all, prostate cancer deaths in the United States have dropped by 20 per cent since the test's widespread use in the late 1980s. Yet, a similar drop also occurred in Britain without any big PSA screening programme.

Not only is there no hard evidence that PSA is useful, the Harvard study also found that many men with a PSA reading under 4, and were therefore not biopsied, actually did have the cancer.

Tumours in 82 per cent of men under 60, and 65 per cent of men over 60, are missed when the threshold for biopsies is set at a PSA reading of above 4.

What is to be faulted is not the test itself but the overly high threshold value.

But how low should the threshold go? Mathematical models showed that if men under 60 were biopsied when their PSA exceeded 2.5, two-thirds of cancers would still be missed. Lowering the threshold even further, however, would cause too many normal men to be biopsied.

For men over 60, a different problem presents itself. The two-thirds of cases with PSA under 4 whose cancers are missed because they are not biopsied, might well be luckier than those who are biopsied because their PSA exceeds 4.

This is because prostate cancers grow very, very slowly, taking decades, so older men may simply die of causes other than the cancer.

Yet, a diagnosis of prostate cancer entails surgery or radiation. Their side effects, including incontinence and impotence, mean a serious deterioration in quality of life.

Given the very low risk of death from the tumour, is this acceptable, especially for older men?

As the authors note: "The big question remains, should we be screening in the first place?" Until on-going studies to address this question are ready in five years, you will have to decide whether the annual PSA test is for you.

In July 2003, though, scientists suggested a simpler way to prevent prostate cancer: *The New Scientist* magazine reported a Cancer Council of Victoria study in Australia which found that 1,259 healthy men who had masturbated more than five times a week while in their twenties were a third less likely to develop the tumour compared to 1,079 men actually diagnosed with the cancer.

Many might wonder — embarrassed guffaws and gratuitous remarks aside — if this is news one could use while waiting for the last word on PSA.

Why anal sex really sucks . . .

WARNING: *This chapter sets out to debunk the myth that gay sex, or more specifically, anal sex is like straight or vaginal sex because the anus is biologically like the vagina and thus as suitable for sexual intercourse. It attempts to set right what is missing in the media's coverage about homosexuality — the all-pervasive blackout or self-imposed censorship on the biological facts that show while the vagina is structurally suitable for sex, the anus is not. This chapter may prove a little scatological for some readers. Gays may find it offensive. If so, I apologise. But these are the facts that will blow away the fallacies. If you are offended, please omit this chapter. But if you want to know why your butt is not made for repeated penetration, and why you can choose not to, please read on.*

SO you are straight but have you fantasised about anal sex with a woman or a man? Or you think you are gay and wondering if anal sex will hurt. Or you could be a gay who has engaged in habitual anal sex and you are now experiencing some problems "down there where the sun don't shine" but get only unhelpful explanations and unfounded tips from your gay friends. Or you are just curious.

Here's the low down on anal sex.

In most societies today, it has become politically correct to not discriminate against gays and lesbians but, regardless of whether you think homosexuality is right or wrong, no one can gainsay the fact that, for the person on the receiving end, (ano-receptive) anal sex is inferior to vaginal sex, biologically-speaking. This is because, while the vagina is superbly structured for intercourse, the anus and rectum are extremely susceptible to internal damage from an invading penis.

Need some convincing?

The rationale for this statement lies in the fact that vaginas differ from rectums in two important ways that can only be discerned under a microscope. The first difference has to do with the different kind of lining either structure has.

To picture what a lining is, think about a modest lady who resorts to a flesh-colour lining under her transparent blouse. In the same way, the linings of hollow organs and glands are made of sheets of cells.

The type of lining is determined by the shape of its cells, whether they are column-, cube-, or scale-shaped. How they pile up upon one another, and the thickness of the layers they pile up to also matter.

While vaginal linings are of one type, the rectal one is another. The vagina is lined by tough flat scale-shaped cells that form thick layers and are piled on top of each other the way a mason builds a thick brick wall.

So there is little leakage through the layers.

Moreover, it secretes a layer of mucus, thus protecting against abrasion and infection. So, even with repeated "insults" and shearing forces from a penis, the top layers of this lining regenerates quickly, bottom up.

By contrast, the rectum — the large intestine's last 15 cm — is lined with a single layer of column-shaped cells that "leak" between one another so that water can be absorbed from the waste before it is passed out.

Because its lining is designed to leak — in contrast to the vaginal lining — any germs introduced through minor tears in the rectum during anal sex can and will seep through into the blood. (The area around the intestines is very richly supplied with blood vessels.)

The upshot of all this?

While the orifices leading into the vagina and rectum may feel the same to an intruding finger or penis, the former repels bugs that come along for the ride while the latter is prone to admit them.

Now the second key difference between vagina and rectum. That difference lies in the muscles next to their linings. The vagina is a tube of muscles. Not single- but double-layered, its stronger muscles run lengthwise on the outside, while weaker muscles run in circles on the inside (next to its strong lining).

By contrast, the anus — the last centimeter of the large intestine — is just a small ring of muscles. It is a one-way valve that normally opens only because of pressure from the inside when the rectum is full of waste. So it is not designed for repeated penetration from the outside. With repetitive trauma and stretching in habitual anal sex, the thin muscular ring will lose its tone and may well leak faeces uncontrollably at the most inconvenient of times. Once past the anus, the trauma gets even worse because the rectum is nowhere near as sturdy as vaginal tissue.

Why?

Because rectal walls have only rings of weak "smooth muscles" that contract rhythmically to push waste along. Smooth muscle, not normally under your voluntary control, are those that give you goosebumps and shrivels a man's scrotum during a cold shower.

Without the surrounding support of skeletal muscles that the vagina has — think of the kind that makes up a slab of beef — the rectum can't protect itself against the friction of penile penetration. Easily perforated, you may not know even if there is large tear as it has no pain sensation, unlike the vagina.

These then are the facts in digestible morsels.

These facts show that, while it may be politically correct to say that each person's sexual preferences is of his own choosing, it is biologically mistaken to assert that anal sex and vaginal sex are the same for all intents and purposes. Biologically, structurally, it's a no-contest: The vagina wins, hands down.

Still unconvinced?

The world is already seeing a second wave of the HIV epidemic and gay men's unsafe sex practices are the biggest cause of the second coming of AIDS.

Gays already know that unprotected sex is risky but they gamble with it anyway. This after effective anti-viral antibiotics that suppress the HIV virus were introduced in April 1996. Called HAART (Highly Active Anti-Retroviral Therapy), they transformed AIDS into a manageable chronic disease, enabling the infected to feel and act well — and resume sex after a period of illness.

As HIV death rates fell dramatically from 1996, many a gay must have developed a false sense of security: If the consequences of risky behaviour seem less severe, maybe you don't have to avoid high-risk sex. Studies show that a third of gays with HIV feel that HAART has made unprotected sex that much more thinkable for them now.

So it is a cocktail of anti-virals that keeps the HIV-positive gay fit enough to cruise around for casual, anonymous and risky sex, thereby spreading his virus and fuelling the second wave.

But remember HAART is no cure: It just keeps you alive. If you keep disrespecting the structure of your rectum and keep having condomless ano-receptive and ano-insertive sex, you are setting yourself up for AIDS which, eventually, is still a death sentence.

The moral: Respect the orifices.

II. Forever young and trim?

Beauty pills — How to distinguish help from hype

HAVE you seen those advertisements in your local papers and on television touting pills that promise to give 40-year-old skin smooth and radiant enough to die for? They could set you back a princely sum every month, though.

The Asian market for these pills is estimated to be US$600 million a year. At S$85–210 per person per month, it is no surprise there are at least five products vying for consumer attention in a market as small as Singapore, say.

Of course, none promises to get rid of coarse wrinkles, sagging skin or a really weather-beaten look. Also, none claims to give you skin like your 10-year-old daughter's either. Rather, they just want to plump out the skin and reduce those fine lines.

So what's new about the pills?

Most skin care products are chemicals that have an effect on the skin's uppermost layer called the epidermis; few can penetrate that to impact the underlying layer, the dermis. Thus, the way for a chemical to get into the dermis is from the inside out, these pill makers argue. They will act from the inside out to bulk up on the dermis' scaffolding made of a magical protein called collagen.

What is this collagen?

A protein made up of tough, long fibres intertwined like small steel wires braided into suspension bridge cables, it has great tensile strength, which is why the collagen scaffolding keeps the skin taut. But skin collagen diminishes as we age. And when we use oxygen to burn food into energy, nasty by-products called free radicals break down collagen. The body's defence comprises scavengers called antioxidants which neutralise free radicals. But some free radicals, unfortunately, will get through, resulting in disrupted collagen — which, over time, leads to wrinkles.

There is another protein in the dermis called elastin that gives young skin its elasticity. After puberty, however, the chromosome that controls its production is switched off, so we stop making elastin. Hence, most attempts to combat skin ageing leave elastin alone: You don't want to mess with switched-off chromosomes.

The only option left is to replenish the collagen but there's a problem: How to get collagen into the dermis?

One surefire, if non-permanent, way is to inject collagen made from animal bone and skin into the dermis. Dermatologists have been using these "fillers" to smooth out wrinkles for decades.

The drawback: Injected collagen doesn't stimulate the skin to produce more collagen of its own. Rather, it degrades and disappears after a few months, so you'll need repeat shots, indefinitely.

If you hate needles, however, you might have to resort to creams and lotions that supposedly bulk up thinning, ageing skin like collagen creams. These do give you the sensation of firmness, probably because they moisturise the skin surface, but collagen molecules themselves are just too large to penetrate the epidermis. They don't work.

Hence beauty pills.

If you look at the list of ingredients on their boxes, you can't miss "hydrolysed collagen" — and numerous botanical extracts that supposedly act as antioxidants.

There are also dozens of ancillary ingredients including vitamins, enzymes, hormones, and almost always substances of marine origin, probably because their DNA resembles collagen DNA.

Here's the lowdown: Despite media attention and consumer popularity that these oral beauty products have garnered, there are few rigorous, peer-reviewed, large-scale human studies published in mainstream medical journals that support their claims to bulk up your collagen and give younger skin.

More positively, some studies show that when some of their ingredients are used in cream or lotion form — but not collgen per se — rather than in pills, they work.

First, there are prescription-strength vitamin A creams (tretinoin). These do lead to the deposition of new collagen, get rid of fine wrinkles, brown spots, and even black heads.

Yes, tretinoin can give the skin a smoother, more uniform texture and a rosy glow, so it is a pity it is underused.

Then, there are natural fruit acids called alpha hydroxy acids. Found in many lotions today, they cause cells in the skin's top layers to become "unglued" from one another, so dead skin cells slough off. This makes room for new skin to grow, so one's complexion improves.

The acids may even stimulate the skin's deeper layers to produce more collagen that keeps skin taut, thus filling out fine wrinkles.

However, they may also cause burning, itching and possibly scarring, especially in those with darker skin. In addition, alpha hydroxyl acids can also increase one's sensitivity to the sun, which leads to sun damage of the skin.

Still, they come at such low concentrations in mass-marketed cosmetic lotions that they are too weak to work. To get results, use 20 to 30 per cent glycolic acid solutions that aestheticians have in their salons, or the 70 per cent lotions or prescription creams that cosmetic surgeons employ.

You'll get moderate improvements in skin texture but peels must be repeated every two to four weeks to maintain results.

So what's not to like?

Such cosmetic products with drug-like effects, called "cosmeceuticals" in industry-speak, that purport to cure rather than merely camouflage skin blemishes may or may not work but there is no guarantee they are safe. Their makers don't have to establish their safety — or efficacy — because most regulatory agencies don't even acknowledge cosmeceuticals as a category, much less regulate them stringently. This means distributors just need to attest that they are safe and ensure that labelling reveals their ingredients.

However, advances in cosmetic technology have blurred the line between cosmetics and drugs: Many may alter skin structure and/or function the way drugs do, but they are not regulated as drugs because they don't claim to treat a certain condition or reduce risks from a specific disease. As cosmetic products, they merely claim to improve one's appearance. Here's the skinny on skin glow products. Problem: Drugs undergo extensive and rigorous pre-market testing for safety and efficacy, but cosmeceuticals don't. One rationale for maintaining the status quo, which focuses on labelling and recalling unsafe cosmetics post-market, might be that many makers do test their products first. This they do if only to avoid product-liability suits and loss of consumer goodwill.

But as the demand for more effective treatments increases, manufacturers may pile on more and more active ingredients, thus heightening the risks to users.

Meanwhile, the law suits we expect disgruntled users to file which would help regulate product safety may not be forthcoming at all because there can always be confidential out-of-court settlements.

These and other concerns mean that the responsible consumer must get the facts right and learn to distinguish help from hype.

Of course, you could always come to terms with ageing skin.

A ray of hope for skin blemishes

WOMEN seeking a radiant complexion must be envious of some 40-something film stars who seem to have perpetually rosy cheeks. How is that possible?

These stars probably try to shed the tired, dry surface layers of their skin so new ones grow to replace them. There are three scientifically tested gizmos to do that if you are as vain.

First, there is micro-dermabrasion that buffs the skin. A special tool propels tiny aluminum oxide crystals against the skin at high speeds to plane off dead surface skin cells which are almost immediately vacuumed away into a handpiece.

The procedure is painless and typically produces only a mild redness but, if performed over-enthusiastically, may cause pinpoint bleeding spots under the skin. The doctor's model delivers more crystals faster, penetrates deeper, sucks the dirt away harder and gives better results than those aestheticians have.

Secondly, there is laser resurfacing which is performed under local anaesthesia.

Your eyes are first shielded, and the area around the face also shielded with wet drapes or crumpled foil to trap stray laser beams. Your doctor will mark off the damaged areas for resurfacing before he begins.

A wand-like handpiece is used to deliver a high-intensity laser beam to vaporise the outer layer of skin (epidermis) bloodlessly — and the wrinkles disappear in a puff of mist.

Next, the laser is used at lower power to heat up the underlying layers (dermis) which stimulates the production of collagen, the protein that provides the skin its support and flexibility. This makes for smoother and tauter new skin. Your complexion is improved and your skin may stay red or pink for up to six months. Fine lines around the eyes, mouth and cheeks can also be removed.

But the procedure also sends you into hiding while you wait for the swelling to subside and the wound to heal.

Laser resurfacing of the face achieves its best results as a spot treatment in the areas of the face where the skin is thicker and has more glands so it is more successful in convex areas of the face. The lateral parts of the cheeks as well as the temples don't do so well.

It may also cause hypopigmentation (or lightened patches), long periods of patient discomfort, and longer periods of reddened skin afterwards.

How long you take to recover depends on what intensity of the laser was used: You'll take longer to recover from deeper treatments. You should plan for about two weeks of recovery time during which you will need medication for pain as well as a steroid to reduce swelling.

Note that if you tend to develop keloids or big, thick scars, or if your complexion is olive or darker, you should avoid laser resurfacing as you are more likely to develop hyperpigmentation (darkened patches) with the treatment.

For everyone else who may receive it and can afford laser resurfacing but can't afford two weeks of downtime, there is now another approach that even beauty parlours in your neighborhood may be advertising feverishly.

Proven in rigorous studies to be effective for specific skin blemishes, the third option is called Intense Pulsed Light (IPL) treatment, a non-invasive method that — unlike lasers — doesn't breach the skin surface. Your face may be slightly pink or red with mild swelling immediately after IPL but this requires almost no downtime at all.

In contrast to a laser which works by producing an intense beam of bright light of one specific colour (or wavelength), IPL uses a wide spectrum of wavelengths for different skin blemishes, so experience is required for proper patient selection.

The IPL handpiece has a smooth glass prism whose surface is applied to the skin to deliver precise pulses of intense light to ageing spots, fine wrinkles, freckles, tattoos, spider veins or even unwanted hair.

Also, since the light is changed into heat energy upon penetrating the lower dermis, new collagen production is stimulated there, which gives you smoother, tighter and softer skin.

The results can be good for people of white European descent but not the dark-skinned. Studies in Hong Kong, Taiwan and Japan that have been published in reputable journals suggest fair-skinned Asians do well, too, and can expect, on average, a two-year reduction in perceived age after each course.

The drawbacks?

Besides being very expensive, it is not the painless procedure that aestheticians make it out to be. Volunteers in a Singapore study conducted by Dr Goh Chee Leok of the National Skin Centre and published in the *Journal of Dermatological Treatment* in December 2003 described a "prolonged burning sensation" — but one that was tolerable.

More important, the increasingly widespread use of IPL worldwide has seen an increase in mistakes resulting in burns, dark scarring or its opposite — overly light or underpigmented patches. Severe burns from IPL have been seen in the dermatologist clinic especially when they are used by untrained doctors or beauticians.

Of course, most beauty parlour advertisements tout the fact that physicians are around or can be contacted during an IPL treatment. But it isn't good enough for the doctor to be contactable: This procedure should be closely supervised to ensure that the patient is not hurt and the supervising doctor must be around the procedure room and be on hand to monitor the procedure.

This begs the question of how aestheticians acquire what is really a piece of medical equipment in the first place. In most Asian countries, there is no statutory control on medical devices. That is so in Singapore, for example.

In other words, you're on your own.

So if you are heading out for a blast of that rejuvenating light but your aesthetician can't supply details of the physician purportedly in charge of her IPL equipment and/or won't assure you that he'll actually be around, you might be better off consulting a dermatologist first.

Or, you might just choose to live with some laugh lines rather than risk bad results on the face where the whole world can't miss.

Hair today, gone tomorrow . . . but science can help

IF you have a hairless pate, a researcher in Singapore claims he has just the thing for you. National University of Singapore professor Lee Chee Wee has tied up with a Hong Kong firm to make and market his Biolyn Hair Serum.

Many are wondering how this lotion, which retails online at US$140 for a five-month pack, actually works. The Biolyn website does not reveal its active ingredients.

According to the maker, it is a plant-based product which prevents receptors in the hair follicles from coming into contact with hormones that cause hair loss. The hair follicle is a small, cup-shaped structure in the skin from which hair grows. Each cup is lined with cells and connective tissue.

A bulbous collection of actively growing cells at the follicle's base constantly produces a strand of hair. The average person has about 100,000 strands of hair on the scalp and loses between 20 and 100 strands a day.

If Biolyn works the way Prof Lee says it does, then its mode of action sounds well within the realm of orthodox science. It is already well known that an enzyme converts the male hormone, testosterone, into dihydrotestosterone (DHT), which damages hair follicles and causes hair to stop growing in men genetically predisposed to it.

Because the enzyme accumulates at the base of the hair follicles across the centre of one's head, this is where most males lose hair.

In the mid-1990s, doctors observed that men with non-cancerous, enlarged prostates who were being treated with the drug finasteride sometimes had hair reappearing on their bald patches. So plans to try it out on baldies were hatched. Tested on 2,000 bald Britons, 80 per cent stopped losing their hair. About 60 per cent even started growing back some hair.

By 1997, finasteride had been approved by British and American authorities as oral medication for baldness.

Sold by Merck under the name Propecia, it is taken once a day, indefinitely, and requires about six months before you start seeing any results. But it does work, and it works well.

However, there is a 2 to 5 per cent chance you may develop some problems that may crush your manhood. These include tenderness and enlargement of the breast tissues, pain in the testes, reversible impotence and loss of sex drive.

It may also cause abnormalities in sperm, so if someone on Propecia wants to father a child, he should stop taking the medication a few months beforehand.

Where Biolyn is concerned, you might not have such worries. One may deduce that this is because while Propecia lowers DHT levels by blocking the enzyme that produces it, Biolyn leaves the enzyme alone, so DHT is still produced.

Biolyn, it seems, will armour-plate those sensitive hair follicles against DHT, or so it claims.

Biolyn also seems to work differently from minoxidil, the only other drug for treating baldness apart from finasteride, and older by about a decade.

Sold by original patent holders Upjohn as a lotion for baldness under the Regaine brand, minoxidil is also found in various "herbal" concoctions, which tend to be more expensive.

Minoxidil was first discovered as an effective hair restorer back in the 1980s, when it was noticed that patients on minoxidil tablets — then used to treat hypertension — grew body hair.

So minoxidil was tried out in lotion form on bald men.

In Upjohn-sponsored trials, Regaine was shown to slow down hair loss in 90 per cent of cases.

Regrowth, however, occurred much less often, and mainly in younger men.

The drug is thought to enlarge hair follicles and stir up resting follicles to get them to start growing. Perhaps it also eggs on follicles that are growing, so they continue doing so for longer periods.

This lotion must be applied indefinitely too.

Its main side effect is scalp itching in some cases. Because minoxidil was originally approved to treat high blood pressure, Regaine should be used with some caution in people with a history of heart problems, dizziness, chest pains or a rapid heart beat.

Newer drugs may be in the pipeline. In March 2004, the *New Scientist* magazine reported that Philadelphia scientists had plucked stem cells from the follicles of mice and implanted them into another animal which then grew new hair. The hope now is to identify the same cells in humans to use in screening for drugs to reverse balding.

Here's the bottomline though. Propecia and Regaine are well-attested therapies whereas Biolyn is not. But whichever you decide to use, there's bad news: As you grow older, your follicles will become even more sensitive to that culprit, DHT. If you ever stop using any of these cures, you will likely start losing whatever you may have regrown.

The older you are, the faster you will lose those precious strands. Nature will always have the last say.

Of grey hair, dyes, risks and hope

IF you are a middle-aged man who has lost your job and you are going to interview after interview hoping to land that elusive job, you would do well to not only bone up on deficient computer skills, but also lose some weight, tone up your body — and dye your hair. After all, like wrinkles and sagging skin, grey hair screams your age out loud.

How do those greys, which spell "washed-out" in these youth-oriented times, get there on the head? And does that Chinese herb called *shou wu* root actually restore hair colour in greying people?

Each strand of hair is made up of the coloured part we see growing, called the shaft, and an end that keeps it anchored under the scalp, called the root.

The shaft is naturally yellow in all races. This, mingling with the specific amount of pigment determined by our genes, gives the various shades of hair colour from blonde to black.

The root of every strand is surrounded by the follicle. This is a pit under the skin surface, shaped like a tube of tissue, that harbours a certain number of pigment cells. These cells produce the pigments which give the growing strand its colour.

Hair grows in length as cells at the base of follicles divide rapidly. As these cells get pushed upwards, they harden and get pigmented to produce a regularly coloured strand.

As we grow older, for reasons still ill-understood, the pigment cells gradually produce less and less pigment.

This happens sooner in Caucasians than darker-skinned people. Thus a white woman starts greying at the sides at, say, 35 years of age while a black woman gets a 10-year reprieve.

Look at your own skin colour and you can work out, in the light of when your mother or father started greying, what age you are likely to start greying.

When there is less and less pigment, the shaft begins to appear white. Sometimes, air bubbles appear in the shaft displacing the granules of pigment too.

We call the white hair grey because that's how it appears in contrast to the regular hair we still have on our heads.

Here's the bad news: This is an irreversible process but people have been trying to fight it for a long, long time.

Even in the first century, greying Romans tried to darken their hair using a dye made by boiling walnuts with leeks.

Until the early 1900s, hair dye was still made in like manner from herbs and plants.

In 1909, French chemist Eugene Schuller created a dye based on a chemical called para-phenylenediamine, which remains the basis of hair dyes to this day.

The following year, his company became the now-familiar L'Oreal.

Though hair dyes today no longer smell like rotten eggs as they did in the past, there are still downsides to colouring your greys.

Hydrogen peroxide, ammonia or lead acetate — the other chemicals used in the hair-colouring process — can be harsh on your hair.

Also, the amine dyes themselves may cause cancers.

An increased risk of bone, bladder and liver cancers, as well as lymphomas, has been observed in some studies.

The risk looks lower than the risk of getting lung cancer if you smoke but the dye-cancer relationship does merit further study.

A better deal may be on the horizon, in the same way balding people have been given new hope by minoxidils — that antihypertensive drug which had the side-effect of regrowing hair on bald patches and is now used to treat hair loss.

While using a drug called imatinib mesylate (Gleevec) to treat leukaemia in the elderly last year, doctors from the Victor Segalen University in Bordeaux, France, noted a strange side-effect.

In 7 per cent of their patients, grey hair became progressively darker within five months.

It is speculated that the drug may block an enzyme that regulates pigment production from tyrosine, an amino acid or the building blocks of proteins.

In 2000, some doctors in Philadelphia managed to restore colour to white hair in albino mice using a cream containing "chimeric oligonucleotides" that have been heralded as promising gene therapy reagents.

These nucleotides employ small hairpin-shaped molecules made up of RNA and DNA to introduce tiny changes into the gene to be modified. In that experiment, the chimeric oligonucleotides presumably helped repair a mutation in the relevant hair-follicle genes. However, as it is a form of gene therapy, if only a cream, doctors have been reluctant to test it on humans.

As for the *shou wu* root, a cousin of buckwheat, it is highly prized in China but not yet rigorously tested in scientific circles.

But you don't have to wait for these tests, or cures. You don't even have to dye your greys. The ancient Greeks bleached dark hair using harsh soaps: For them, lighter hair denoted courage and honour.

Eating less to live longer?

WHAT has starving got to do with longevity?

There is now a lot of research on how restricting one's calorie intake retards ageing. It is not about becoming anorexic or starvation unto malnutrition. Rather, eating a nutrient-dense diet with as little as two-thirds of the typical calorie intake may enhance human longevity. And this "undernutrition without malnutrition" approach may also keep debility and disease at bay — though death will still come eventually. This according to scientists like Dr Richard Weindruch from the University of Wisconsin.

But mum always said to eat up, so where did the idea come from?

In the 1930s, Cornell University scientists found that rats placed on a diet with 30 per cent fewer calories lived a third longer, from three years to four. They also suffered fewer late-life problems like heart disease, diabetes, cancers, cataracts and deafness.

The experiments have been replicated successfully many times. If you extrapolate mice results to humans, that is extending average life spans to 110–115 years, the maximum currently observed.

Tried out in the 1970s with yeast, fruit flies, worms, fish, spiders, mice and hamsters, caloric restriction was found to work in these species as well.

However, long-term projects in primates — rhesus and squirrel monkeys — began only in 1987. These are still under way but interim observations suggest they respond the same way too.

The projects will have to go on for another decade or so before scientists really know if the calories-restricted group outlives control groups of free-feeding monkeys. (Rhesus monkeys live about 24–40 years; squirrel monkeys, about 19–28 years.)

In human subjects?

The only unplanned, scientific evidence for humans comes from four men and four women who spent two years — from September 1991 to September 1993 — in a tightly sealed ecological space called Biosphere 2. (Earth is presumably Biosphere 1.)

In the experiment conducted on 1.2 ha of desert near Tucson, Arizona, the eight had to grow their own food but, as the yield was less than projected, they were forced into a calorie-restricted diet of about 1,800 calories per person per day. This was quite little in view of the physical labour.

Though in his later 60s then, the resident physician, Dr Roy Walford, who was Dr Weindruch's mentor, was not spared the toil either.

At the end of the experiment, all eight had lost weight but were otherwise healthy. They showed the same lowered levels of blood sugar, cholesterol, insulin, cortisol and blood pressure that mice have on a similar diet.

Though there were no sex- and age-matched controls to compare them with — so it did not count as a rigorous caloric restriction study — the findings suggested that the regimen may retard ageing in humans. (Sadly, Dr Walford, who was planning to live to 150, died in 2004 of a neurological disease. He was 79 years and 10 months old.)

So how does drastically cutting calories without skimping on essential nutrients work?

A key player in ageing may be oxidation, a process not unlike rusting. The body uses oxygen to burn up food and, during this process, the oxygen is also converted into very unstable molecules called free radicals. These react rapidly with proteins, DNA and lipids, generally causing ultimately permanent damage to tiny power stations inside our cells called mitochondria.

Over time, this makes for less efficient metabolism. Reducing the overall amount of fuel (calories) coming into the body for processing means a lighter load of free radicals and, thus, less cellular damage.

Nothing simpler than popping anti-oxidants daily to stay younger then?

We do not know the answer to that yet. Vitamin E, for example, is widely pushed by industry as an anti-oxidant that mops up free radicals but there is no rigorous proof that it retards ageing. Vitamin E certainly can't get into the brain, which has a specialised barrier to keep out any germs that might be in the blood while permitting oxygen in.

A better approach is to look for a drug that mimics the effects of caloric restriction. One candidate is deoxyglucose, which lowers mitochondria activity so that fewer free radicals are formed. It causes the same changes in blood chemistry as caloric restriction does but it has to be used at near-toxic doses to be effective.

Another candidate without deoxyglucose's toxicity is iodoacetate, which is now under study.

A third and even more exciting possibility is resveratrol, a chemical compound long known to be found in red wine that first gained recognition as the reason why the French who have a predilection for lots of fatty food yet have a 30 per cent lower incidence of heart disease than Americans, and why just 7 per cent of French adults are obese while 22 per cent of Americans are. Resveratrol is an antioxidant found in a number of plants, including grape skins, raspberries, mulberries and peanuts. It helps fight fungus during the rainy season, and it is especially prevalent in grapes used in making red wine. But recently, resveratrol has been identified as an agent that replicates the effects of caloric restriction.

By 1992, resveratrol had been shown to protect imbibers against heart disease and other ageing-related illnesses. By 1997, resveratrol had been shown to have potent anti-cancer effects in mice as well. And now this. In 2003, Harvard University researchers showed that resveratrol can extend the lifespan of yeast, roundworms and fruit flies. For example, yeast lifespan was extended by 70 per cent, on average.

Resveratrol acts by stimulating a class of enzymes called sirtuins — which laboratory mice put on a low-calorie diet have 50 per cent more of than those fed normally. (Animals, and probably humans, produce more sirtuins during stressful periods such as food scarcity.) What an excess of sirtuins does is to suppress a protein called BAX that causes cells to commit suicide. In experiments with human cell cultures, resveratrol stimulates sirtuins which then retard cell suicide within 24 hours. In short, red wine could increase our longevity.

That's the good new — so why don't I take resveratrol which is already available in pill form?

The bad news is it gets oxidised away very easily in the same way that, once a bottle of red wine is uncorked, oxygen in the air begins to break down the resveratrol so that any wine kept overnight will have little of it left.

Well, maybe a small bottle of burgundy regularly may yet do the trick.

These are early days yet but what caloric restriction shows is that ageing can be retarded. Yet, many in the science establishment look askance at such research, which suffers by association with the quacks who hawk the many putative elixirs of youth. So it remains unpopular and under-funded. But it is very important science and should be funded.

Atkins, a dieting delusion?

ONCE upon a time, whether you ate too much of anything, the excess carbohydrate or protein or fat meant extra calories that went down to the waist line.

Yet a study claims that you may eat more and still lose weight — if you eat very little carbohydrate but a lot of protein and fat. This small study of 21 people, done by Harvard University and reported at an American Association for the Study of Obesity meeting in October 2003, showed that such dieters lost even more weight than those on a standard low-fat diet.

Over the 12-week study period, these so-called Atkins dieters even ate 300 calories more per day. These should have tallied up to 3 kg on the bathroom scales — but they didn't.

Can you really eat more on a low-carbohydrate diet and yet lose as much or more weight? Over the past year, several studies have shown that compared to the standard low-fat diet, people on an Atkins diet lost more weight, at least initially.

The first multicentre study of the diet was published in *The New England Journal Of Medicine* in May 2003, which showed that, in the first six months, Atkins dieters lost twice as much weight as those on a standard low-fat diet.

At the end of one year, however, both groups had regained enough weight so there was no statistical difference between the two groups.

What was special about this study, though small, was that all meals were prepared by an upmarket Italian restaurant. What dieters were getting was known with precision unlike most other studies where dieters are entrusted with following a set menu on their own.

Favoured by celebrities, the Atkins diet allows the dieter unlimited amounts of proteins and fats but carbohydrate intake is restricted strictly. Food such as bread, rice, potatoes, pasta, fruit and starchy vegetables are shunned in favour of protein-heavy food such as meat, eggs, fish, bacon, meat and cheese.

The late Dr Robert Atkins first published his *Diet Revolution* in 1972, which put forward an argument that contradicted the overwhelming majority of then-existing research on how to lose weight safely. It made a comeback in December 2001 as the *Dr Atkins New Diet Revolution.* Already 11 million copies in print, the book blames carbohydrates for weight gain, so the diet cuts out virtually all of it.

Under these conditions, for energy, the dieter's body burns up carbohydrates already stored as glycogen in the liver and muscles. Many people get hooked because there is a rapid initial weight loss. This weight loss however doesn't come from body fat. It comes from water. For every gram of glycogen that the body stores, it must store 3 g of water. When glycogen is broken down, stored water gets excreted — lots of it — so weight loss appears magically on your scales.

However, Dr Atkins argued that carbohydrates over-stimulate the production of a hormone called insulin, provoking hunger, more eating, and thus weight gain. Insulin invites body cells to store fat, he said, so if you cut the carbohydrates, you avoid high insulin levels, and you'll drop the kilos.

But it is untrue that only carbohydrates stimulate insulin production: All ingested food stimulates insulin production. Insulin enables our cells to take up glucose from blood and use it for the energy we need to do everything from thinking to running a triathlon.

Yes, insulin does help the body to store fat, but it is untrue that it does so only when carbohydrates are eaten. Fat is stored if too much of any food is eaten.

If the body takes in fewer calories than it uses in a day, all those calories will be used for energy. If the body takes in more calories than it burns, insulin stores those extra calories as fat.

Either way, it matters not where the extra calories come from. If they come from carbohydrates, the body turns the extra carbohydrate into fat which gets stored. If extra calories come from fat, they can be immediately stored as fat. To blame insulin is junk science.

The Atkins diet disallows grains, fruits and vegetables, which might predispose the dieter to cancer and heart disease.

The high-protein intake is also disturbing. In balanced diets, proteins are digested into amino acids while waste products get filtered from the blood and excreted.

An overly high protein intake may strain the kidneys' ability to deal with the extra load of waste products. A Harvard study published in a prestigious journal, *Annals Of Internal Medicine,* in 2002 showed that 489 of the 1,624 women whose high-protein diets were monitored for 11 years showed some deterioration in their kidney function.

So what to make of the Harvard finding on Atkins dieters mentioned above? It seems to defy a basic law in physics that you can't take in more calories and yet lose more weight — unless you are burning more off.

Perhaps, the group exercised more or they ate less. Whatever the case, the study needs to be replicated on a much larger scale for a much longer period before people start gorging themselves on proteins and fats while abstaining religiously from carbohydrates.

While its claim is interesting, it should not detract from the more important question, which is whether the Atkins diet is harmful in the long run.

A multicentre, five-year United States study going on at the universities of Pennsylvania, Colorado and Washington should answer this very question. Pending its results, it's best to regard a fad as just a fad.

Best carb blocker? Look in the mirror

THE diet industry likes to use drop-dead gorgeous, lissome leading ladies as its alluring poster girls. But before you sidle up to them, watch out: The svelte ladies might also have lots of, er . . . gas — if they take diet pills called "carb blockers". Whether they work or not, these blockers could induce nausea, abdominal churning and bloating.

Suddenly, carb blockers are everywhere, probably because faddish diets like Atkins' have turned people against carbohydrates ("carbs") or starches, so the idea of taking a pill that prevents carbs from doing their dastardly deeds is a surefire way to sell. If they are to be believed, one or two tablets with a meal will block the absorption of hundreds of calories from starchy food like rice, noodles, bread or potatoes.

How do they work their magic?

The pills contain a protein derived from the white kidney bean that supposedly slows down starch digestion, so that it passes through you largely undigested. This protein allegedly works by binding to and interfering with amylase, the enzyme your pancreas produces to break starch down into a simple sugar called glucose that is small enough to be absorbed into the bloodstream.

As your blood glucose rises after a meal, your pancreas also cranks out insulin, a hormone that signals body cells to absorb the glucose and burn it off for energy, or store excess glucose as fat for future energy use. Unfortunately, stored fat means you pile on the kilos. Hence take carb blockers to stop the enzyme that starts it all, purveyors reason.

So this is the latest in the fight against flab?

Well, no and yes.

In the early 1980s, another extract from the same bean was touted as a "starch blocker" too. That extract was hydroxycitric acid (HCA), on which a pharmaceutical giant called Hoffman-LaRoche (now Roche) had spent millions researching as a weight-loss drug. However, the effort was abandoned — precisely because HCA didn't work satisfactorily.

Nevertheless, diet-pill makers picked it up and began selling HCA as a weight-loss aid.

By 1982, the United States Food and Drug Administration (FDA) had received more than 100 reports of abdominal pain, diarrhoea and vomiting from users of starch blockers. The agency then drove starch blockers from the market.

Those blockers had no significant effect on both starch metabolism and blood-sugar levels, because people produced a lot more amylase than they could block. The little bit of starch that actually got away undigested reached the large intestine already fermented, which caused the gas and bloating.

In 1994, however, a new US law reclassified many diet preparations as nutritional supplements, not drugs. This meant the FDA could only prosecute makers in the event of adverse reactions in actual use or if grossly false claims were made for their products.

Asian regulators have generally taken the same tack, so the same food supplements can flood Asian markets too. For example, Extrim is a US product; Xando from Norway can be found in many Asian cities today.

So blockers have reappeared in new garb.

Today's blockers claim to have the real thing, of course. Also extracted from the same bean, it is a protein called phaseolamin. This time around, some makers say that double-blinded studies — the gold standard in clinical trials of new drugs so there is no patient or doctor bias — have been done to prove their carb blockers do work.

Really?

Advertisements for Extrim, for example, claim that, among others, a chemistry professor at the University of Scranton, a small college in Pennsylvania, did such studies in 2001. However, these haven't been published, which means we don't know if they can stand up to peer review or expert scrutiny.

The chemist, Dr Joe Vinson, declines to share his unpublished data when asked.

Also, a tiny study this year (of 27 people) by University of California at Los Angeles dons doesn't support the claims. Funded by another carb-blocker manufacturer, the work was published in an obscure journal, *Alternative Medicine Review,* that isn't included in the mainstream US National Library of Medicine database.

Yet even these authors concluded the weight loss with phaseolamin wasn't statistically different from a placebo. The advertisements don't point this out, of course.

Meanwhile, the marketers will permit you to view these largely unpublished clinical studies only on their premises. That, to say the very least, is highly unusual as far as scientific evidence goes, especially since phaseolamin isn't even a prescription drug.

If these studies look iffy, the FDA has stated that there is no new evidence carb blockers work as claimed. In March 2004, it even warned a US firm marketing "Ultra Carbohydrate Blocker 2000" to desist from making the usual carb-blocker claims which, the agency said, "are not supported by reliable scientific evidence".

Yes, researchers at the renowned Mayo Clinic in Rochester, Minnesota, did a small unpublished study recently which showed that very high doses of phaseolamin do slow down starch digestion — but such doses are not available in commercial carb blockers.

So here's the skinny on carb blockers: There is no credible evidence they'll work for you.

No worries, though: You are the best carb blocker ever.

Why?

Because you can choose what to move from your dinner plate to your mouth.

Before you try rolling away your cellulite . . .

YOU might have seen those posters outside slimming salons, depicting a woman reclining in a white body stocking while an attendant kneads her hips with a set of hand-held mechanised rollers. Endermologie, it is called, the deep mechanical massage in which many a woman has come to pin her hopes in the fight against cellulite.

The word Endermologie is derived from "ende" (under) and "derm" (skin). Endermologie's main bragging right, highlighted in these posters, is that it is "FDA-approved". (The Food and Drug Administration or FDA is, of course, the regulator of drugs and medical devices in the United States.)

The company that pioneered Endermologie is always careful to state that it doesn't remove cellulite but merely reduces its appearance.

Many want to know if it works but let us begin first with cellulite — the lumpy-bumpy dimpling of the skin around women's hips, buttocks and thighs.

It afflicts women more frequently than men. When men get it, it tends to afflict their neck and abdomen, rather than the hips or buttocks. The industry claims that up to 80 per cent of women have cellulite. If true, that is a potentially huge market for cellulite-busting outfits and remedies, effective or otherwise.

Cellulite has been described as orange peel skin or cottage cheese skin. Coined by the French salon and spa industry, "cellulite" itself isn't even a scientific term. The condition, however, was long recognised and described in detail by European physicians early in the 19th century but was popularised in the English language only in 1973 by *Cellulite: Those Lumps, Bumps and Bulges You Couldn't Lose Before,* a book penned by one Nicole Ronsard who owned a beauty salon in New York city. Since then, studies have shown that cellulite is made up entirely of ordinary fat cells whose biochemistry and physiology are no different from fat cells elsewhere. That is, cellulite is not a uniquely different kind of fat. What is unique, though, is how the pattern of connective tissue immediately below the dermis, or the second layer of the skin, differs between the sexes.

In the female, at sites on her body where there is cellulite, a high percentage of the connective tissue below the dermis is thickened bands running perpendicular to the skin surface. These create tall, thin boxes that extrude fat tissue into the dermis, giving rise to dimpling. Except for these vertical bands, connective tissue below the dermis in females is irregular, discontinuous and diffuse. In women with cellulite, a 2002 Rockefeller University study using the MRI scan showed, the inner fat layer is also greatly thickened as well.

By contrast, in males, the same layer of connective tissue is smooth and continuous, running diagonally against the skin, so it presses down on the fat, keeping it smooth. The cause of these differing patterns between men and women is not known. What is known is pesky cellulite doesn't respond to weight loss, exercise and creams.

Can it be rolled away, then?

Originally developed in France in the late 1970s to soften burn scars, the Endermologie massager seemed also to improve body contour and skin texture in some patients. The massager has two small motorised rollers and a suction device. Suction lifts the skin — the hope is to stretch the fibrous bands so they become more flexible and pliable — while rollers knead and massage the underlying fat, perhaps improving blood and lymphatic flow. Body suits are worn to reduce any direct contact with the skin so there is no skin irritation.

Usually, six to 14 sessions — each lasting 30 to 45 minutes — are advised. These are followed by one or two treatments a month to maintain results. Today, both doctors and aestheticians use the rollers. Any difference in results may well depend on who is wielding the contraption. Pressures achieved in the underlying fat have been measured with probes under the skin and shown to be highly dependent upon the therapist. This was proven in a Vanderbilt University study published in 2001 in *Plastic and Reconstructive Surgery,* a mainstream journal, where the pressure exerted on cellulite by the Endermologie rollers was measured with probes under the skin.

Other reputable studies show that the treatment increases blood and lymphatic flow within the skin. For example, a study published in the *Aesthetic Surgery Journal* in 1999 showed that Endermologie exerts an easily measured but profound effect on the body's physiology — whether or not it actually changes the body contour. For example, it causes a four-fold increase in the blood flow of veins within the skin's fat and a three-fold increase in its lymphatic flow.

Also, women who have failed to menstruate for a period may see their menses return after regular Endermologie sessions. Another study in the *Aesthetic Surgery Journal* in 1999 documented this. Changes in the levels of female hormones in the blood were also detected during and after the sessions.

These findings suggest that the Endermologie massage may exert its effects by altering the physiological and metabolic activity of fat, which are really active tissues that produce hormones and such, not just passive stores of calories as had been taught until recently. Unsurprisingly, massaging fat may produce various physiological changes in the body — whether it redistributes fat cells anatomically or not; whether the rhythmic folding, unfolding and suction actually changes body contours or not.

But is this equipment FDA-approved?

As usual, the truth is a little more complicated. The Endermologie massager was classified as a Class I medical device, which meant that the manufacturer's claim that it temporarily reduced the appearance of cellulite didn't have to be substantiated. The relevant US law states that as long as a new device is "substantially equivalent" to a similar device in use before May 28, 1976 — such as a variety of inexpensive cellulite massagers with rubber tips and wooden balls — the manufacturer may market it without waiting for FDA approval.

The reality then is that Endermologie was exempt from meeting FDA approval, not FDA-approved as such.

So should it be used?

Some studies find it effective, others not. Someday there might be a machine that gives permanent results but the Endermologie is not that miracle machine.

Since cellulite is purely a cosmetic issue, not a disease, the issue really boils down to whether you can afford the treatment: The first 14-session course of Endermologie costs about US$1,000 in most Asian cities.

Then there are maintenance visits.

Just do the math and decide if you can afford to lose so much dough for so little fat.

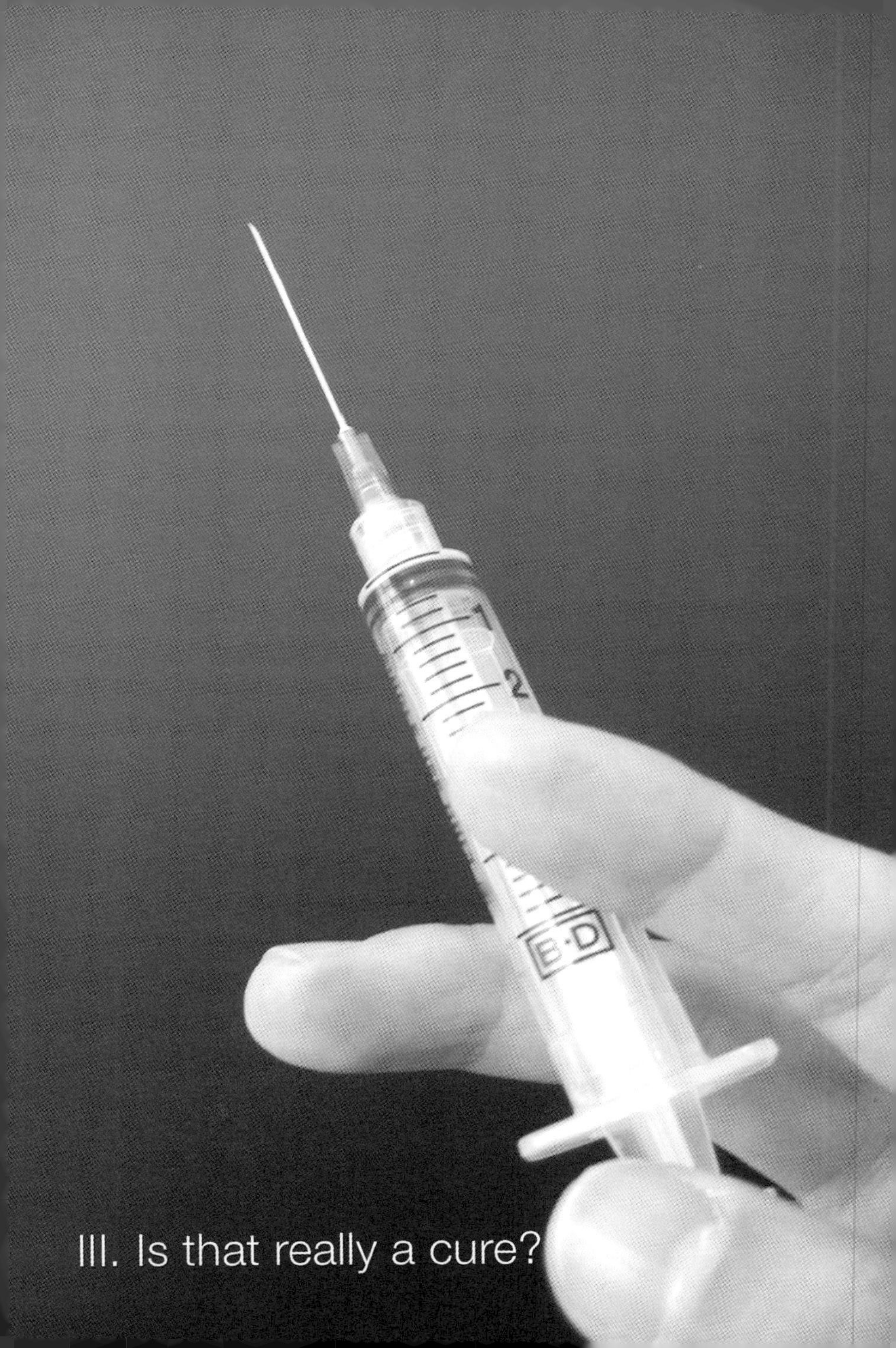

III. Is that really a cure?

More muck than magic in a colon flush

IN many prosperous Asian cities, scumbags from the West are pedaling "wellness" programmes that include something called "internal cleansing". On the premise that disease and death begin in the colon, regular washing out of the large intestine or colon is said to "detoxify" the body, thus promoting one's general health.

It sounds reasonable to many as people already believe that "regular" bowel movements are crucial to health because they think stagnation of feces in the colon can lead intestinal bacteria to produce toxins, which then enter the body through the gut wall. The large intestine is pictured as a sewage system that becomes a cesspool in the constipated. Others say constipation leads to hardened faeces accumulating on colon walls, thus preventing their proper functioning.

Advocates say toxic residues cause a multitude of problems, from menstrual pain and migraines to sinus congestion and poor concentration, from gas and bad breath to body odour and parasitic infections. Thus, constipation is to be avoided. The folk saying that an apple a day keeps the doctor away is rooted in the idea of increasing roughage to speed up the elimination process.

It goes back much further: In antiquity, the Egyptians made the same connection. The Greek historian, Herodotus, noted that "for three consecutive days in every month they (the Egyptians) purge themselves, pursuing after health by means of emetics and drenches, for they think that it is from the food they eat that all sicknesses come to men".

This theory of "intestinal autointoxication" actually held sway in 19th century medicine, which led surgeons in the early part of the 20th century, chief among them a famous Scottish surgeon Sir William Arbuthnot Lane (1856–1943), an eccentric who thought of humans as machines, to perform total colectomies — surgically removing the whole colon — as a cure for auto-intoxication.

On the other side of the Atlantic, Dr John Harvey Kellogg (1852–1943) tried to reshape the colon surgically to secure more rapid evacuation. He also developed peanut butter, granola, and toasted flakes to help bowel movements, poor one being, he claimed, the cause of 90 per cent of all illness. Kellogg's fame made the bowel a national obsession in the US. After each breakfast, he would have an orderly give him an enema but the rich and famous came to his sanatorium to get their bowels cleansed more thoroughly with gallons of water introduced from below — colonic irrigation — that was finished off with a healthy serving of yogurt up the same route.

Between 1919 and 1922, the theory was disproven in a series of experiments. Yes, irrigation machines were commonly found in US hospitals and physician offices up to the 1930s but they fell out of use as the underpinning theory was discredited within scientific circles, The idea, however, has persisted in the public mind, probably because of early childhood toilet training. Thus some may resort to enemas or laxatives to induce what they think is regularity.

But now a resurgence of interest in and popularity of colonic irrigation, first in the US, and now here, probably as part of a widespread postmodern interest in complementary/alternative medicine. This procedure that readers have called up about involves infusing large quantities of distilled water at body temperature into the colon via the anus to wash away years of accumulated muck and mucus, practitioners claim.

Up to 50 liters may be mechanically pumped in over an hour, say. (By contrast, an ordinary enema introduces only 100–200 cc, and that into the rectum only to help get hard, impacted faeces out.) Some providers use an apparatus where the water flows in more gently by gravity only. Other liquids may be used too, including coffee, wheatgrass extract, and so on.

In practice, while you lie on your side, the operator inserts — or you may self-insert — a suitably lubricated kiddie-sized plastic speculum into the rectum. (Alternatively, you may adopt the knee-chest or doggie position, with your chest touching the couch.) The operator then introduces two tubes into the speculum, one to let clean water in and a bigger one to let used liquid out. All the while, the abdomen is massaged to stimulate colon movement and the effluent is channeled into the toilet.

Feeling queasy already?

By now, you might be wondering who would agree when someone says: "Can I interest you in a few gallons of lukewarm water up your rectum?" or let someone else probe them "where the sun doesn't shine", except in the context of a doctor's examination? Well, the late Princess Diana did. The Royal Flush, three times a week, she said, was her secret to health and beauty. Apparently, some folks here are believers too, since the business seems flush with clients.

Some people actually get psychological or physical pleasure from colonics and some even become addicted to them or the feelings they have as a result. They maintain this "high" for a time until they again feel toxic and have to "detoxify" via another colonic. In the United States where home kits can be purchased — in fact they are available over the Internet — a large proportion of buyers are male homosexuals, some of whom find erotic satisfaction in using these devices.

But here's the skinny on the procedure the Queen of England pooh-poohed as distasteful and disgusting: Not merely useless but also potentially dangerous, colonics represent, as a wit said, a triumph of ignorance over science.

First, the symptoms of constipation have nothing to do with intestinal toxicity at all. In the early part of the 20th century, a researcher managed to replicate those symptoms — dry mouth, tiredness, lassitude, and so on — by simply packing the rectum with sterile cotton.

Second, there is simply no need to irrigate the colon because the entire lining of the colon is regenerated and replaced every day, so residues and toxins can't accumulate on intestinal walls. Most of digestion and absorption of nutrients occur in the small intestine and the waste that remains enters the large intestine, where water and minerals are extracted before waste is passed on to be eliminated.

Third, colonic irrigation systems are medical devices that doctors use to prepare the colon for examination with X-rays or with colonoscopes, flexible fiberoptic telescopes physicians use to look inside the colon. The patient must first formally consent to the procedure, including the colonic preparation, having understood the risks and benefits of the procedure before it is done.

No irrigation system has been designed for routine use by untrained people to promote one's general health. The tubes may be passed up the colon rectum for a distance of some 50–60 cm. Some cases of punctured bowels with contaminated colonic equipment leading to septicaemia (blood poisoning), electrolyte (salt and mineral) depletion, and heart failure caused by excessive fluid absorption have been reported.

Last year, for example, one death and four perforated colons occurred in Texas following colonics. On July 6 two Texan manufacturers of the device, and a colonic irrigation service provider admitted to unauthorised use of such systems without physician involvement. The equipment makers agreed to permanently go out of business, while the provider agreed to pay penalties and court costs after the Texas state government sued.

What should you do?

The fallacy behind irrigation is that without a daily bowel movement, your health is endangered. Normality, in fact, varies from three times a day to three a week: Whatever has been your normal is normal. Conversely, a change in bowel habit may be abnormal. The colon is self-cleansing and no build-up occurs. If you eat a high-fibre diet, drink plenty of water and exercise, your colon will keep itself clean and in working order. You can't flush your troubles away but then you don't need to.

Coffee cure for cancer? Add a pinch of caution

CONTINUING our story about "detoxification", it is a historical fact that the late Princess of Wales, Lady Diana, once confessed to having coffee enemas, saying they purified her system.

The enema is an ancient medical procedure in which a fluid is injected into the rectum to clear out the bowel. This serves to relieve constipation or prepare the bowel for surgery, X-rays or endoscopy.

Coffee enemas are for a different purpose altogether, and they will be available in some Asian countries like Malaysia but not others like Singapore where authorities have taken a stand against them.

The Gerson Institute plans to open a centre in Malaysia where the highest Malaysian authorities have given the go-ahead for this project. However, cancer patients in Asia who hear about this, and their families who may understandably be willing to try anything, need to be circumspect about the regimen, including the enema.

Developed by Dr Max Gerson, the therapy involves a special diet of organic food with supplements claimed to stimulate metabolism and coffee enemas to cleanse the body.

After he died in 1959, his daughter, Charlotte Gerson Strauss continued the therapy, which is currently available only at The Gerson Institute in Tijuana, Mexico. The clinic claims a high cure rate for cancers but makes no data public.

The charges there are US$6,000 for a three-week stay but Malaysia hopes to offer it at half that price, or less.

Proponents say fertilisers, insecticides, and herbicides contaminate food by lowering their potassium content and raising the sodium content. This changes cellular metabolism and leads to the "accumulation of numerous damaging factors... slow poisoning of the entire organism... and weakening of the liver, the prime organ of detoxification, (and thus) cancer", Dr Gerson had suggested.

The remedy, fans say, is a no-sodium diet with lots of high-potassium fruit and vegetables, typically juiced, to correct the sodium-potassium imbalance.

To revitalise the liver, injections of liver extract, oral pancreatic enzymes and various supplements are also given.

Then, there is the coffee enema to eliminate toxins. An apparatus that relies upon gravity introduces a boiled-then-cooled solution of organic coffee through the anus into the colon.

Proponents claim that Vitamin B3 in coffee beans dilates bile ducts in the liver, thus helping the organ excrete more toxins into the intestines. When the colon is evacuated, the toxins are carried out of the body, it is claimed.

The coffee enema appeared as early as 1917 and was found in the prestigious *Merck Manual*, a compendium of orthodox medical therapies, until 1972. So coffee enemas were an established part of medical practice when Dr Gerson used it for "detoxification" first in tuberculosis, then cancer.

However, there are no peer-reviewed studies to date that show any benefit from coffee enemas in cancer therapy.

One doctor, Nicholas Gonzales, while a medical student, was inspired by Dr William Kelley, who had treated the 1960s Hollywood superstar Steve McQueen's lung cancer with coffee enemas.

Dr Gonzales began a study on treating pancreatic cancer with coffee enemas in 1999 at the Columbia College of Physicians and Surgeons in New York City. He chose pancreatic cancer because only 4 per cent of patients live five years or more, with 80 per cent dying in the first year. In the United States National Cancer Institute's largest study of 126 patients on conventional treatments, none survived beyond 19 months. In Dr Gonzales' pilot study, two patients lived for four years and one for almost five. The median survival time was 17 months.

Although he had looked at only 11 patients, the data could not be ignored and the US National Institutes of Health gave him a US$1.4 million grant to start trials.

This was a coup for an alternative treatment but, four years into the study, he does not have the 90 patients he needs for his trial. The reason is oncologists are not falling over themselves to refer their patients to the unusual programme.

The procedure is not risk-free either.

Patients have had their bowels perforated.

If too much of the solution is held for too long in the bowels, excessive fluid may be absorbed into the bloodstream causing electrolyte (salt and mineral) imbalances and even heart failure in the frail or the elderly.

Despite criticism from the medical establishment, Dr Gonzales is playing by the rules as he tries to validate the treatment by adhering to the scientific method and working within orthodoxy — in contrast to the Gerson approach.

Patients in Asia who want to use the Gerson facility in Malaysia should know that there is, as yet, little support within conventional medicine for coffee enemas.

While awaiting Dr Gonzales' study to be completed, they must do so with their eyes wide open.

Cure for cancer? Don't start drinking urine yet

SOME time in 2004 a reader of mine rang me to say that her neighbour's child had a brain tumour and she had heard that drinking urine might help. Would I look into it?

My thoughts immediately flitted back to Mr Morarji Desai who was India's prime minister when he stunned everyone in 1978 by admitting to a lifelong habit of drinking his own urine every morning — for health reasons.

He did live to be 99.

I managed to suppress a guffaw because I had just read an article in the March 2004 issue of a journal, *Integrative Cancer Therapies*, that dealt with a report about an aborted study about using a compound called antineoplaston in fighting brain tumours.

Here's the link: Antineoplastons, a word derived from the Greek "for anti-cancer", were first extracted from urine.

Made up of amino acids bonded together in a certain way, antineoplastons are also found abundantly in blood and various organs. In the early 1960s, Rockefeller University scientists had discovered them in healthy individuals. In 1968, an immigrant to the United States, Dr Stanislaw Burzynski, now Texas-based, noted that antineoplastons were absent in cancer patients.

Perhaps they prevented cancers from developing in healthy people, he postulated. If you don't have enough of them, perhaps that's when cancer strikes.

If true, they could be used to cure cancers.

Since then, Dr Burzynski has made antineoplastons his speciality, and set up a clinic in Houston using them to treat cancer patients. He says roughly a third of his patients with brain tumours respond completely or partially, a third remain stable or unchanged, while a third don't respond, so they deteriorate.

This response rate stands in stark contrast to conventional chemotherapy and radiotherapy, with cure rates in brain tumours of under 1 per cent in all cases.

So from December 1991, the US National Cancer Institute (NCI) began testing the compounds but four years later, the study was terminated without ever establishing a definitive answer.

Dr Burzynski's supporters alleged the NCI wanted to use the trial only to discredit antineoplaston therapy, while NCI supporters claimed that

Dr Burzynski didn't want the trial to proceed as it would show antineoplastons to be quite useless.

However, the March 2004 report I was reading found something less sinister.

The falling-out had come about mainly because of interpersonal conflict and communication failure, with both parties being insensitive to each other's "face" needs.

So we still won't know if drinking urine helps?

Right off the bat, it is unlikely that a patient with a brain tumour will get enough antineoplastons, assuming they work, by drinking urine. To extract enough for one patient, about 120 litres of urine have to be processed, which is why the Burzynski Clinic has been synthesising antineoplastons in its own private plant for years now.

But do they really work?

Detractors point to the prematurely terminated trial, whose scientific findings were reported in a mainstream journal, *Mayo Clinic Proceedings,* in 1999: It had only nine patients, of whom six could be evaluated for response. All six showed no tumour shrinkage. All nine patients died before the study closed, with only one death directly attributable to cancer.

Although the authors said "because of the small number of patients in these trials, no definitive conclusions can be drawn", the results were clearly extremely disappointing. Dr Burzynski is still allowed to use antineoplastons in terminal cases that have already received conventional therapy, but he must report each case to the authorities regularly. But independent reviewers have found several fundamental problems with his studies.

First, anyone who comes through the door with any type of cancer is included.

Conventionally, clinical trials define strictly what diagnoses may or may not be included so we know if the therapy works for a specific cancer.

Second, he collects data in an anecdotal manner.

His annual reports to the authorities present only raw data: Charts with patient information, response to treatment and current status. All brain tumours are lumped together, whereas they are conventionally treated according to their microscopic appearances.

When he reports changes in tumour size, it is unclear who reads his brain scans.

Third, there are no helpful summary statistics or discussion of his results. In general, Dr Burzynski presents a morass of uninterpretable data. After nearly three decades, his results haven't been published in a meaningful way, so antineoplaston efficacy remains unproven and unapproved for routine use.

Diehard fans say that's because there is a conspiracy to keep "natural" products out of the market: Naturally occurring substances can't be patented. Freely available, they would erode the profit margins of the giant pharmaceutical companies, they say.

In fact, basic economics leads to similar results — without the need for a conspiracy at all. How?

Any new cancer therapy must undergo extensive and expensive clinical trials before approval. These and other developmental costs can rack up a bill of US$300 million for each drug that makes it to the market — which freezes out anything but the giant corporations.

So a non-patentable therapy, even if safe and effective, is unlikely to make it to the market. Antineoplastons could well be such a candidate, but unless Dr Burzynski's research shapes up, there is little reason to emulate the late Mr Desai.

Flushing out clogged arteries

"WHY can't doctors just flush out the muck clogging up my heart's arteries?" many a heart attack survivor has asked. Truth be told, in the near future, they just might be able to, what with a new treatment in the offing — and the economics being about right.

Since the late 1980s, drugs called statins have been the mainstay of treatment. These gradually lower the amount of fat in the blood stream. Because fats get deposited on the inside of arteries to clog them up, lowering fat levels whittles away the gung.

Reducing fats by half cuts down heart attacks and deaths by a quarter to a third. But that's slow and patients are condemned to a life sentence of statins — and bland food.

Yes, flushing the plumbing clear would be nice, but it's a mere pipe dream. That's because of the constraints imposed by the way the body processes cholesterol, the waxy artery clogger.

Cholesterol is moved around in the bloodstream all wrapped up in proteins to form packages called lipoproteins. As everybody knows, there are two kinds of cholesterol. First, there's the "bad" cholesterol in low-density lipoproteins (LDL) packages. To date, therapy has focused on reducing these.

Then, there's the "good" cholesterol in high-density lipoprotein (HDL) packages, a major component of which is called Apolipoprotein A-I (ApoA-I). The master key to cholesterol removal, ApoA-I scours the gunge and carries cholesterol from it back to the liver for elimination. That's why you just can't get enough of HDL.

More HDL, less gunk. Less HDL, more muck.

If that seems like a no-brainer, why is there no HDL therapy? In a word: Economics. Since HDL (or, more specifically, ApoA-I) exists only in nature, it can't be patented, so no company will fund its study or development as a drug.

There is evidence that vitamin B3 (niacin) might increase HDL levels. But since niacin is freely available in milk, nuts, cereals, legumes and green leafy vegetables, and can't be patented, no drug company will spend time and money proving it works.

Losing some weight, throwing away those cigarettes, and drinking red wine in moderation may raise your HDLs somewhat, but really high levels are for the fortunate few with the right genes, just the luck of the draw.

Until now.

This is thanks to one man born in 1780 in a picturesque hamlet in northern Italy called Limone sul Garda, just outside of Milan. Two centuries later, one of his descendants would be found to have very low levels of HDL (with high levels of another bad fat called triglyceride). Yet, his arteries were like squeaky clean pipes. What's more, he had 40 other relatives with the same unique condition. All traced their ancestry to that one man who gave them an unusual mutation in the gene that makes ApoA-I.

That mutated gene enables them to produce a different Apo, called ApoA-I Milano, that clears up clogged arteries faster than you can say "Jumping Jack Flash".

The cardiovascular health and longevity of this group of 41 intrigued scientists from the University of California at Los Angeles (UCLA), who found from lab tests that their Apo particles could bind cholesterol twice as efficiently as garden variety Apo.

When the Milano Apo was isolated and injected into mice and rabbits with clogged arteries, sure enough, the animals' plumbing cleared quickly.

Sceptics, however, pooh-poohed the theory, arguing that since the purity of the isolate could not be assured, there was no way to prove it worked. That was in 1979.

Today, genetic engineering would come to the rescue and make a pure Apo so that the theory could be tested once and for all.

But this called for funding. Money came — because the mutant gene that makes the Milan Apo could be patented. (Normal genes like that which makes the garden variety Apo can't be.)

An American firm in Ann Arbor, Michigan called Esperion Therapeutics, which owned the rights to the gene, genetically engineered some pure ApoA-I Milano for animal tests. When these were successful, it proceeded to human trials.

Between November 2001 and March 2003, it carried out a small but rigorous trial involving 47 people admitted to ten United States hospitals for acute chest pain caused by clogged heart arteries.

The trial was double-blinded, meaning both doctors and patients didn't know whether they were receiving the real thing or a placebo. This eliminated patient and physician bias.

When the results were published in November 2003 in the *Journal of the American Medical Association*, they caused a tremor in the community of heart specialists.

The findings were dramatic: On average, the drug caused 4 per cent shrinkage in the volume of clots in the coronary arteries after only five weekly injections. The shrinkage of nearly 1 per cent per week was ten times faster than anything any cardiologist had ever seen before.

The UCLA scientists who had made the original discovery were the only ones not too taken aback, having seen similar results in their animal studies.

On the basis of this trial, the giant drug firm Pfizer bought over the Esperion firm for US$1.3 billion on Dec 22, 2003, according to Dr Steve Nissen of the Cleveland Clinic, who led the trial.

With Pfizer's unlimited R&D resources, a large-scale trial involving 5,000 to 7,000 people is in the offing, he added.

It looks like a whole new way of treating the killer illness — flush out clogged arteries and clear the disease quickly — may really be at the door, thanks to genetic engineering.

Chemical "claw" the answer to clogged arteries?

CONTINUING our story about flushing out blocked arteries in people with atherosclerosis, or thickening and hardening of artery walls, some doctors say that bypass surgery is not the best option for the condition as it can strike any artery.

You need something that works system-wide to clear the gunk from all and not just the coronary arteries, they say. Blocked arteries other than in the heart can also be serious; for example, a bad case of blocked arteries in your legs — that's peripheral vascular disease — may mean amputation.

So what do these doctors suggest?

Chelation therapy.

This involves infusing patients with an anti-coagulant found in some test tubes which doctors use to collect blood samples. Called EDTA, for ethylenediaminetetraacetic acid, it, proponents suggest, removes from circulation loose metal ions that are involved in oxidation.

Such oxidation triggers off various reactions that end up damaging artery walls, leading to atherosclerosis. EDTA also inhibits enzymes called metalloproteinases that help form the gunk in your arteries.

The chemical is given in a slow drip over three to four hours, in an outpatient setting. There are usually 20 to 30 treatments.

First synthesised in Germany in the 1930s, EDTA is an organic chemical — an amino acid with four molecules of acetic acid attached to it — whose molecular structure has a claw of sorts. The term chelate comes from the Greek chele, for claw. This claw enables EDTA to pick up and bind calcium, for example, so it was used in the 1930s to remove calcium from pipes and boilers.

Because its claw can also pick up heavy metals like lead, mercury and cadmium, when EDTA is injected into the blood it binds such metals and allows them to be excreted in the urine. Indeed, it is approved for treatment of heavy metal-poisoning in people.

But it is not approved for use in coronary artery disease or peripheral vascular disease, which is what some 800 doctors in America and a handful in Asia use it for.

So is there any evidence that it works?

Very little if you scour mainstream publications. After all, this is off-label prescribing, or using an approved drug for conditions other than those for which it is officially sanctioned.

For example, aspirin, an approved painkiller, was used for years to reduce repeat heart attacks before that use was sanctioned. As experience accumulated and data was analysed, this off-label prescription was proven effective and authorised.

EDTA hasn't been as lucky.

Over the last 40 years, there have been only five studies reported in mainstream journals that are cited in Medline, the online database of the United States National Library of Medicine that researchers worldwide depend on. By misinterpreting their own published data, all five studies concluded that EDTA is no better than a placebo.

For example, a 1994 New Zealand study published in *Circulation* showed that non-smoking subjects walked an extra 325 m without pain after EDTA treatment. Meanwhile, subjects given a placebo could only muster an extra 225 m. That's a 44 per cent difference but the authors concluded the placebo was equally good.

In 1996, a corrected analysis of its data showing statistically significant benefits from EDTA was published in *Alternative Therapies*, a mainstream journal, after *Circulation* refused to publish the correction. Their methodologies were also suspect. For example, a small Canadian study, published in the *Journal of the American Medical Association* in January 2002, recruited participants, a third of whom had no angina, or chest pain, to test a drug that purports to treat angina.

The subjects were also given other angina drugs. This is a fundamental flaw as no drug authority would ever approve a new drug tested in a trial where subjects did not discontinue all other drugs for the condition completely.

The striking incongruities in all five studies published in the best journals and the dearth of studies could suggest there might well be a certain animus towards chelation therapy in mainstream medicine.

Can the Gordian knot be cut?

Since EDTA can't be patented, no drug company will ever commit resources to prove it works but, late last year, the US government began funding a US$30 million, five-year study at 100 US hospitals. This project will eventually involve 2,372 heart attack patients — 20 times bigger than any previous study — so it should settle the issue.

If proven to work, it could help reduce mortality rates from heart disease and strokes. If shown to be ineffective or harmful, hopefully doctors will stop using it. We will see.

Take heart, red wine still best for coronary health

IT is well known that the French have a low incidence of heart disease despite a relatively high fat diet. Scientists speculate that this might have something to do with their habit of quaffing lots of red wine.

In fact, by the early 1990s, a chemical found in wine called resveratrol had been identified as possibly the molecule doing the trick.

To date, a lot of animal experiments indicate that resveratrol combats "bad" cholesterol which damages the heart. Specifically, it quenches free radicals, those particularly reactive atoms that can start chain reactions which lead to cell damage.

When bad cholesterol is acted upon by free radicals, it leads to hardening and narrowing of arteries (atherosclerosis). Resveratrol helps scavenge the free radicals and terminates the chain reactions before atherosclerosis worsens.

Where is it found?

The most abundant natural source of resveratrol in the Western world is the fruit of the vine, though it is also found in plant species like lilies, mulberries and peanuts. It occurs in the vines, roots, seeds and stalks of the grape plant but is most concentrated in grape skin (not flesh).

Red wine has more of the molecule — almost ten times more. This has to do with how long grape skins are present during fermentation. Red wine is fermented with grape skins left on for much longer while for white wine, the skins are removed early in the process.

It also depends on where the grape is grown because resveratrol belongs to a class of compounds that plants produce to fight stresses such as cold weather, fungal attacks and lack of nutrients. Since fungi thrive in colder, wetter climes, grapes grown in such localities have more of the magic molecule.

Thus resveratrol appears most in red wines produced in cooler areas with more disease problems, like Burgundy and New York, rather than warmer, drier climates like Australia or California. In a recent Cornell University study of 111 United States and foreign red wines of 1995 vintages, those from the northern state of New York had the highest resveratrol concentration.

Does this mean that health is as close as the nearest bottle of red wine?

Not necessarily.

Besides heavy drinkers having higher rates of nerve disease as well as brain, oesophageal, liver and breast cancers, there is no guarantee your red wine has enough of the molecule.

First, as mentioned above, resveratrol content varies widely depending on where the grapes are grown, so those from harsher northern climates do better. However, because insecticides and fungicides are almost invariably used, the plants are not stressed by disease very much. This means they produce little of the molecule anyway. What you really need is organic red wine produced without the use of fungicides or any other chemical.

Secondly, once a bottle is uncorked, even if it is an organic Burgundy, oxygen in the air begins to break down the resveratrol so that any wine kept overnight will have little of it left. You may drink it all each time you uncork a bottle but this could be a slippery slide into alcoholism.

What's an imbiber to do?

As luck would have it, there is a more stable and concentrated source in an Oriental plant called *hu zhang* or false bamboo, a member of the buckwheat family that goes by the scientific name of *Polygonum cuspidatum.*

Its roots far exceed grape skin in resveratrol content.

Predictably, the nutritional supplement industry has already been marketing lots of resveratrol pills, putatively *hu zhang* root extracts. These are made mainly in China and the US but it is technically very difficult to standardise concentrations of the active molecule.

Moreover, its breakdown on exposure to oxygen during extraction and storage in ordinary containers that are not vacuum-sealed makes the product shelf-life questionable. Remember, nutritional supplements are not considered drugs, so they are unregulated. This means you may not be getting the 100 per cent resveratrol the label promises.

But if you don't mind genetically-modified food, there may soon be a resveratrol-enriched lettuce in Asia. Associate Professor Chia Tet Fatt of the National Institute of Education in Singapore has inserted into the red leaf lettuce the very gene from grapes that makes resveratrol.

Since it is leafy, this lettuce makes many times more of the molecule than grapes do.

What if you are a health-conscious person and you don't trust genetically modified food — or the supplement industry?

Then imbibing organic red wine occasionally may be your best bet.

For now.

A "shock machine" at home may just save that life

IF you have a heart patient in your family, what you must secretly fear most is seeing him or her collapse without any warning at all. Heart patients have been known to clutch their chests, keel over and die.

Though people often call this a heart attack, in medical terms, it is really a cardiac arrest. That is, after suddenly developing an extremely irregular heartbeat called ventricular fibrillation (VF), the heart just stops functioning as a pump effectively.

The frightening thing about cardiac arrests is they can occur without prior warning. By contrast, there is always chest pain and other complaints before a heart attack strikes.

Heart attacks occur when coronary arteries that supply blood to the heart muscles are blocked, causing some of those muscles to die off. The heart then begins to function badly as a pump.

In VF, by comparison, no blood gets pumped out to the body at all. This is because the heart's powerful lower chambers, called the ventricles, begin beating — fibrillating — 400 to 500 times a minute, so fast that the heart feels like a wriggly bag of worms if you hold it in your palms.

After five seconds of this ineffectual pumping, with no blood going to the brain, the patient begins to lose consciousness. For every minute that the heart stays in this mode, the chances of surviving drop by a drastic 10 per cent.

A controlled electric jolt to the heart, however, may change things. It causes the heart to stop beating all together for a short while, and then to resume beating at a normal rate and rhythm.

Delivering that shock is called defibrillation, and the gadget, a defibrillator.

If performed successfully within two minutes, there is an almost 100 per cent chance of surviving. Do it at seven minutes and the figure drops to under 30 per cent.

So time is of the essence and immediate availability of a defibrillator is the determining factor of survival.

So why not make them more widely available in the community? Several US cities including New York City and Los Angeles already have automated defibrillators publicly available in government buildings, shopping malls, fitness clubs, cinemas and so on. There, research shows that the lay public — protected from legal liability by law — have used these widgets to save many lives. Italy,

Sweden and Canada, among other nations, have had similar experiences.

In Asia, they are already available at Changi Airport and on all of Singapore Airlines' commercial flights.

In November 2003, an American Heart Association conference reported that a huge study in progress already shows that non-medical volunteers — using automatic defibrillators plus cardiopulmonary resuscitation (CPR), the kiss of life — saved victims twice as often when cardiac arrests occurred in public compared to those who administered CPR alone.

If true, why not have home sets? After all, many cardiac arrests occur at home where someone is likely to be around. A US$30 million study begun by the US National Institutes of Health in May 2003 aims to settle this specific question but results are not expected until 2007.

Too long to wait?

If it is well within your means, it may not be all that foolish to get a home set, especially if you have one or more risk factors like obesity, hypertension, diabetes or high cholesterol levels which are conducive to coronary heart disease. In 70 per cent of cases, VF occurs in those with coronary heart disease.

In such patients, VF can be triggered by medication, physical or emotional stress, and electrolyte imbalance. Young victims may have diseased heart arteries or muscles in their medical backgrounds.

VF can also be the first — and last — manifestation of heart disease in those with no known risk factors. Unfortunately, 75 per cent of all patients die before they reach a hospital.

Today's home defibrillators are easy-to-use, accurate and fail-safe. Two studies using mock cardiac arrests showed that even 11-year-olds and over-65s, respectively, can operate the device faultlessly after only minimal instruction.

This is because these devices have a huge ON button you can't miss. You flick that on and apply the paddles to the chest, one high up on the victim's right chest, the other to his left, near the armpit.

The machine then analyses the rhythm: If it is VF, a verbal prompt tells everyone to "stand clear" and the operator to then push the "shock" button. It then checks the rhythm again and tells you whether another shock is needed.

Though doctors may be reflexively sceptical about a machine reading heart rhythm patterns, the computer on board looks only for VF; it does not interpret fine nuances.

Studies show that it is 99.9 per cent correct when it says VF is detected and 97 per cent accurate when it says VF is not detected.

What if no shocks were advised, but the button was pushed anyway?

Have no fear: The device will not deliver the shock. Unlike the professional models, these home models have no manual overrides. The bottomline: If your risk profile merits it, or if your financial profile allows it, having a home set looks like an insurance policy worth the price tag.

An "oil" for arthritis?

WHENEVER his joints locked up, all Tin Man had to do in The Wizard Of Oz was to lube them with a few drops of oil, and all would be well. If only life were like fiction!

When our joints become arthritic, the physician generally prescribes painkillers as he has, in fact, no drug that can actually reverse the disease process.

So it piqued the interest of some when a National University of Singapore researcher, Dr Lee Chee Wee, began recently to market a glucosamine cream he had developed for osteoarthritis.

Osteoarthritis, the most common form of painful joint disease, afflicts many over 60. It is often caused by physical injuries, repetitive joint stress, and an inherited predisposition.

So would glucosamine help?

It just might.

The basic problem in an arthritic joint is that its cartilage is degenerating relentlessly.

Cartilage is a porous, elastic, gel-like material that cushions the ends of bones and acts as a protective shock absorber. A clear, sticky substance called synovial fluid fills the joint space and serves to lubricate and nourish the cartilage. All these are packed together in a water-tight capsule surrounded by muscles and ligaments.

Because of this structure's cushioning and gliding qualities, we don't suffer bone-on-bone contact every time we move. (Bone-on-bone contact is what happens in arthritis and can be excruciatingly painful.)

Think of joints this way: If you squeeze a water-filled balloon very hard, the pressure gets transmitted from side to side as the water re-distributes itself. Likewise, when we walk, jump or run, cartilage and synovial fluid respond together to the pounding by re-distributing the load evenly.

But cartilage must stay nourished enough to serve these functions. Since it has no blood supply, it must depend on nutrients dissolved in the synovial fluid to keep it in good working condition.

Two of these nutrients are especially important. First, collagen — the stuff injected into faces to fill wrinkles out — forms a mesh-like work that acts as the skeleton.

The second is proteoglycan — starch attached to protein — which absorbs a lot of water and swells like a sponge to fill the collagen mesh-like work and make the cartilage elastic.

Thus, the resiliency of cartilage depends primarily on proteoglycans. Here's where glucosamine comes in: It is needed to make proteoglycans. Glucosamine itself is glucose (sugar) linked to an amino acid, the building block of all proteins. In osteoarthritis, there is inflammation within afflicted joints which uses up glucose, so there is not enough of it to make glucosamine.

The spongy stuff inside the collagen mesh then becomes like a dried-out sponge so the cartilage is rendered weak and unable to take the pounding from our walking, running or jumping.

The cartilage then progressively degenerates, which is the main feature in osteoarthritis.

Given all this, it stands to reason that arthritis could be reversed if you can deliver enough glucosamine to the afflicted joint.

Though the logic is sound, there is not enough high-quality or long-term research to determine if ingesting glucosamine is efficacious and safe. Glucosamine is widely available as a dietary supplement. As it is not a prescription drug, and thus not subject to stringent drug approval processes, the rigour of glucosamine studies and their conclusions or claims need to be carefully scrutinised.

Understandably, then, the medical community has been sceptical about glucosamine — until recently. A careful review of studies now suggests that it does help to relieve pain and, perhaps, even regenerate cartilage already lost in arthritic joints.

What happened to change the fraternity's collective mind?

In January 2001, for the first time, a respected medical journal — *The Lancet* — reported a three-year-long study in Belgium involving 212 osteoarthritis patients who were given either glucosamine or a placebo, orally.

Significantly, this was a double-blinded study — the gold standard of drug trials — meaning that neither doctor nor patient knew whether the latter was taking glucosamine or the placebo. Double-blinding eliminates physician and patient bias.

In the study, the symptoms of patients in the glucosamine group improved by 20–25 per cent compared to those on placebos. Even with some technical controversies about whether the cartilage itself had re-generated or not, this was a groundbreaking study.

However, all other glucosamine studies done to date have been either too small, too short, or merely focused on pain relief rather than cartilage re-generation.

To settle the question once and for all, the United States government is funding a comprehensive long-term double-blinded study of oral glucosamine therapy for 1,588 osteoarthritis patients.

Begun in 2000, its final report is due in 2005. In the meantime, available data seems to suggest glucosamine may help those with osteoarthritis.

How best to use it then?

Most glucosamine is sold as capsules or pills, although some research suggests that the liquid form may deliver more of it to the bloodstream. In both cases, though, much is broken down in the stomach and lost. To avoid oral intake altogether, Dr Lee chose to try to deliver it through the skin instead. By "hiding" glucosamine molecules within oily envelopes so they do not break down in the cream base, the resulting product may deliver through skin more glucosamine into blood than a similar oral dose.

The sad thing is this ointment did not undergo clinical trials before marketing so there is no proof that it works so people could be "oiling" their joints — and getting well, with life imitating art.

As it stands, glucosamine pills may be a better bet.

Right to ban *ma huang* supplements

WHEN my late grandmother had a cold, she would steadfastly refuse to take pills like Actifed, Contac or Sudafed. For her, it was a Chinese herb called *ma huang* — or bust.

Little difference, we thought: The active ingredient in *ma huang*, called ephedrine, or one of its derivatives, was exactly that in most cold preparations. But ours were pills you could pop.

Grandma, whose own grandfather was a herbalist, often said "Western pills" were toxic. It is true their ingredients may include polyethylene glycol, which sounds like radiator coolant, or something equally ominous like "FD&C Blue dyes 2 and 3". Grandma much preferred a special mixture of herbs, floridly named *Xiao Qing Loong Tang*.

She said it was an ancient formula with *ma huang*, cinnamon, dried ginger, peony, licorice and some other herbs I can't recall now. She would get it from a Chinese medicine shop and boil the herbs down with water into an evil-tasting decoction, then imbibe it with great difficulty and disgust. Often, she would be well the following day, seemingly faster than us with our cold preparations.

How did *ma huang* work its magic?

Grandma, who was a teacher, always explained that *ma huang* "moved water" by facilitating "the flow of *lung qi*". She said all the herbs in the prescription, except the peony, were "warm-natured" so they caused fluids to circulate and evaporate, thus alleviating her congestion. Peony supposedly modulated *ma huang*'s potency.

Though her explanation sounds fanciful now, she may have been right about the peony. *Ma huang*'s safety record when used in combination with other herbs in the traditional way is a good one. By contrast, since its epiphany as a Western dietary supplement, it has been associated with adverse reactions, including fatalities. Grandma would have been scandalised.

The cause of the dubious transformation?

Unpredictable dosages.

In excess, ephedrine, the herb's main active ingredient, may cause nausea, vomiting, palpitations, dizziness, nervousness and seizures. Importantly, it can raise one's blood pressure and heart rate and cause heart attacks or strokes.

However, in appropriate dosages, ephedrine works by constricting blood vessels in the congested linings of breathing passages. This dries up any watery discharge and opens up blocked noses, which is why it works on colds.

The stark difference between *ma huang (Ephedra sinensis)* used as a herb in the traditional way and *ma huang* in capsule form comes about because its ephedrine content varies wildly with species and place of origin.

There are about 40 related Ephedra species which may be found in India, Iran and other areas, but *ma huang*, specifically, is indigenous to China. Little ephedrine is found in its roots. Instead, it is concentrated in the stem.

Many herbalists agree that its dried stems are much safer to use than extracts because the former's pedigree is known. By contrast, it is impossible to monitor the safety level of each batch of the extract in supplements. Often, the ephedrine content in supplements differs markedly from their label claims, and may even approach dangerous levels.

Because their ephedrine content is not standardised, you don't know your intake. Thus, the United States Food and Drug Administration (FDA) has banned all dietary supplements containing *ma huang*.

The plant itself, as used in traditional Chinese herbal remedies, is exempted.

Cold preparations with synthetic ephedrine, or derivatives, are also exempt since they are of known potency.

This ban could not have come too soon. Reports of adverse reactions from their consumption, even deaths, had been escalating since the mid-1990s. These rose in tandem with the industry's aggressive marketing of *ma huang* formulations for weight loss and athletic performance, among others.

The products range from capsules to powders, energy bars and energy drinks. Many have words like "thermo" or "fat burner" in their names, while others don't. They can be bought here from independent distributors or over the Net. But their claims are unsupported by the science.

Yes, ephedrine has a molecular structure akin to amphetamines, which can help one lose weight by suppressing appetite. But ephedrine doesn't have that effect.

The research done to "prove" *ma huang* (alone or in combination with caffeine and/or aspirin) can "burn fat" — which led to a booming business in *ma huang* weight-loss products — has been of poor quality.

True, the ephedrine molecule also resembles adrenalin, the body's natural stimulant that prepares us for "fight or flight" when facing danger.

Ephedrine drives up one's heart rate and blood pressure and, while milder than adrenalin, lasts ten times longer.

Even so, there is simply no scientific evidence that these effects, or others, can enhance athletic performance. Yet, they are pushed extensively with promises of slimmer torsos and unbounded athleticism — all without the hassle of a doctor's appointment.

Sadly, a gullible public identifies herbal products as "natural" and, by extension, healthful or harmless. Add that belief to the unregulated status of dietary supplements and the potential for *ma huang* abuse is high.

So the ban makes sense.

Grandma told us her grandfather said *ma huang*'s nickname was "army general" — powerful and effective if deployed correctly, hazardous if abused.

He was quite right.

Spirulina — Pond scum or wonder food? Jury's out

POND scum may cause liver damage.

That is, a health supplement called spirulina may cause your liver to fail.

Not a few Asians have now taken to this blue-green algae, hyped as "so low on the food chain it has to be packed with nutrients and energy — and it is!".

Fans say spirulina is so rich in protein, vitamins, minerals and other beneficial nutrients, it is "nature's perfect food, capable of sustaining life without the need for other foods".

Yes, it has eight essential amino acids and high levels of vitamin B, beta-carotene, calcium, iron, magnesium, manganese, potassium and zinc.

Yes, it contains vitamin B12, otherwise found only in animal meat — but humans cannot absorb its B12.

The Aztecs ate spirulina as a food called tecuitlatl, if records kept by the Spanish conquistadors are to be believed. The Kanembu people of Central

Africa have harvested it from Lake Chad from ages past, and eat it as sun-dried cakes with a salsa dip.

As algae reproduces very quickly and individual plants stick together, spirulina is easy to harvest, so fans call it "a food source to nourish the world's population".

True, dried spirulina is 70 per cent protein by weight, but the United States Food and Drug Administration (FDA) says that the claim is meaningless: You will need to consume many mouthfuls of expensive spirulina capsules in order to get enough protein every day this way. It is easier and cheaper to get the protein by eating grains or meat — and to get iron from dark greens, or carotenes and vitamins from common fruits and vegetables.

Spirulina is taken as a powder mixed with water or in tablet or caplet form. It is purportedly good for medical conditions ranging from cancers and high cholesterol to AIDS and obesity.

Very preliminary evidence from very small studies suggests that spirulina — like other nutritious plant foods — may help in some of these conditions.

But the findings have yet to be confirmed by larger and longer studies.

Spirulina consists of one or more members of a family of blue-green algae, with some characteristics of bacteria and some of algae.

Under the microscope, it appears as a blue-green spiral of long, thin threads.

Blue-green algae grows in shallow, warm, slow-moving or still lakes, accumulating on the surface as blue-green scum that, at high enough levels, makes the water smell and taste bad.

Out of the 1,500 species of blue-green algae, a few — such as spirulina, chlorella and aphanizomenon flos-aqua — are popularly used in supplements.

Not unlike cultured table mushrooms being safe while wild ones can be poisonous, most types of algae appear to be non-toxic.

So what's the problem?

Some varieties produce microcystins, or toxins made up of amino acids, the building blocks of proteins. The problem is that these toxins may contaminate the algal supplements which you buy in health stores.

In 2000, the Department of Health in the US state of Oregon surveyed 87 commercially available blue-green algae products and found 85 of them were contaminated with microcystins.

How toxic are microcystins?

In February 1996, when a haemodialysis clinic in Caruaru, Brazil, used untreated water for dialysis during a water shortage, about 60 out of 100 patients with kidney failure died. The cause: The water was contaminated with microcystins.

That was dramatic but unusual.

More generally, microcystins accumulate in the liver over the long term and cause toxic problems. Evidence from China suggests a link between microcystins in drinking water and primary liver cancer.

In 1999, after several blue-green algal products were found to contain microcystins, Canadian health authorities sampled those being sold. They found that only products which were made from spirulina blue-green algae harvested from controlled ponds contained no microcystins.

Other blue-green algae such as chlorella and aphanizomenon flos-aqua harvested from natural lakes contained microcystins in excess of World Health Organisation standards.

True, cultured spirulina can be grown free of microcystins, and consumers deserve products that are certified to be toxin-free.

Spirulina is commercially grown in large ponds that depend on sunlight to evaporate the water off. Yet, how much toxin other algae may produce while in the water and how much toxin, if any, is present at harvesting cannot be predicted, as it depends on environmental factors such as the amount of sunlight, depth of water, minerals in the water and time of harvest, among others.

Contamination levels will thus vary from batch to batch.

This makes it difficult to assess the risk in each brand, and even different batches of the same brand. Screening each and every batch calls for phenomenal resources.

To compound the problem, there are different levels of toxicity in microcystins, varying according to their molecular structures. The means used to elucidate molecular structures are only available in research institutions.

Since spirulina is a food supplement and not a prescription drug, it is not subject to the same strict regulations that cover the latter. Makers do not have to declare fluctuations in toxin levels, how they monitor them, and if they do it consistently with every batch.

So because of the potentially variable composition, and until there are rapid, sensitive and reliable tests available for microcystins, a reasonable rule of thumb when you reach out for that expensive bottle of spirulina seems to be: Think pond scum.

Why green may not be everyone's cup of tea

ASIA has it good when it comes to cancer, it would seem. Asian males are much less likely than their American counterparts to have prostate cancer. The population in China has a lower risk of gastric cancer than the West. Japan has a low rate of lung cancer despite its high rate of smoking. What one factor may account for all this? Green tea, some say.

The Asian habit of drinking green tea supposedly prevents problems ranging from caries to cancers, from heart attacks to skin ageing. Not surprisingly, green tea has morphed into green tea toothpaste, skin-care products, shampoos, even perfume. It seems you can't go wrong with green tea.

Yet, today, what is preferred here and in the West is black tea, which comes from plucked tea leaves that are partially dried, crushed and then allowed to ferment or oxidise in dry heat for a few hours. However, this processing leaves black tea with less of certain active substances called polyphenols.

(Animal studies show polyphenols have 100 times the antioxidant punch of vitamin C, so they may help ward off cell damage and, possibly, cancer. Fermentation oxidises away these antioxidants.)

By contrast, green tea, which comes from the same plant, is consumed primarily in China, Japan, North Africa and the Middle East. To stop the fermentation (oxidation) of plucked leaves so they remain green, they are steamed at high temperatures, which deactivates the digestive enzymes lurking within them. The colour of the leaves is thus preserved — the deeper the green, the higher the grade — and the polyphenols remain intact.

So, how to get all that polyphenol goodness?

Tea leaves must be steeped in hot water for at least three minutes so all the polyphenols end up in your drink. Fresh tea leaves have lots of polyphenols called catechins, a kind of tannin that dissolves in water and gives tea its astringency.

This is why green tea is not everyone's cup of tea. But if you haven't yet acquired a taste for green tea, you may not have to. Researchers from The Chinese University of Hong Kong report in the June 2004 issue of the *British Journal Of Nutrition* that canned and bottled tea drinks have as much polyphenol as the hot brew itself.

However, the real question is whether one should even bother. More pointedly, does green tea prevent cancer?

True, tests show polyphenols can prevent solid tumours developing in mice. Yes, a specific catechin called epigallocatechin gallate (EGCG) can cause cancer cells in cultures to die. But large population studies of humans have shown mixed results.

For example, a study conducted by scientists from the Shanghai Cancer Institute and the US National Cancer Institute (NCI) in 1994 found that non-smokers who drank green tea habitually were 60 per cent less likely to develop cancer of the esophagus or gullet. On the other hand, a recent review of 35 subsequent human studies on colon, urinary bladder, stomach, lungs and esophageal cancer found mixed results.

So no one really knows for sure.

While no large clinical trials have been completed at this time proving or disproving the theory, there are randomised clinical trials sponsored by the NCI going on at various US universities.

Meanwhile, a few cups a day won't do any harm, right?

Perhaps.

But as some studies suggest, you may need ten cups a day or more to get discernible benefits. At that level of intake, you will also load up on fluoride. Fans like to say green tea also prevents caries because of its high fluoride content but this is because tea leaves accumulate so much more fluoride from soil and air pollution than any other edible plant.

Over the past 20 years, the fluoride content in green tea has frequently exceeded the maximum level allowed in drinking water.

Here's the problem: Excessive fluoride intake may promote cancer of the bones (osteosarcoma) and the uterus. Even if it doesn't, fluoride inhibits polyphenol activity, thus possibly robbing tea of its cancer preventive activity, if any.

Then there is the caffeine in tea.

Even if coffee has three times as much, the excessive caffeine in tea is enough to cause anxiety, tremors and insomnia. More important, caffeine makes fluoride even more available in the body, thus augmenting its effects. Moreover, aluminum also found in tea enhances the potential of fluorides to cause nerve and kidney damage.

All this points to a possible reason why population studies show varying results: Green tea contains volatile oils, vitamins and minerals in addition to polyphenols, fluoride, caffeine, aluminum and so on. All these compounds may interact together in complex and cumulative ways in the body, quite unlike the straightforward ways polyphenols behave in isolation in laboratory experiments.

Finally, there is also the problem of pesticides used in tea cultivation. The increasing seriousness of this problem was red-flagged by the European

Union (EU) in July 2000, when it ratcheted up the number of pesticide residues that can be found in imported tea it wanted tested from seven to 134.

The following year, China's tea exports to the EU fell by 37 per cent. Last week, Morocco, which accounts for one-third of China's green tea exports, announced it may adopt EU standards soon.

So you still want that cuppa?

Go organic — until China, which produces 90 per cent of the world's green tea, gets its act together.

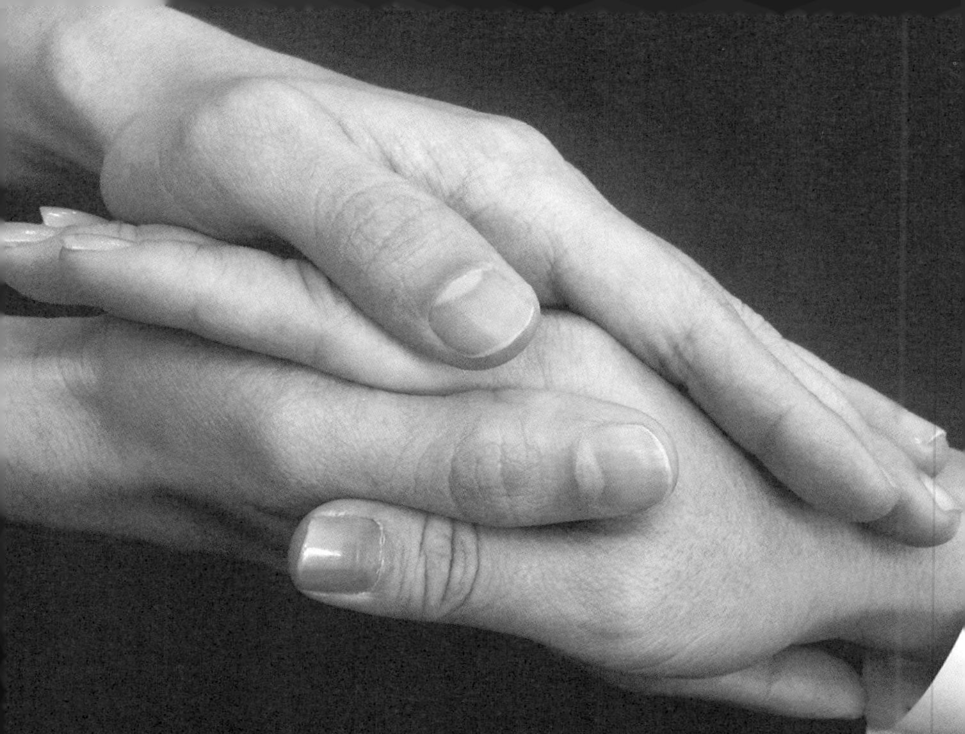

IV. You're sure, Doc?

Doctor, can I really trust you?

IF money now plays a bigger role in the practice of medicine, as many of us cynically take for granted, how can you tell if your doctor is really telling you what is medically warranted or if financial considerations are driving his advice?

I found myself asking this after I was warned that if my cholesterol levels got any higher, I might need to take drugs called statins — for life.

That being the case, I thought I owed it to myself to make sure that the lipid hypothesis, which says that elevated levels of animal fats in the blood cause coronary heart disease, was indeed true.

I turned to the literature only to find studies I had not been told about which suggested, instead, that it is modern diets that are high in hydrogenated vegetable oils like margarines — not animal fats — that could be the culprits responsible for the dramatic rise in heart disease and cancer from the 20th century.

Some studies even detailed how the edible oil industry had used money to influence lawmakers

IV

and the medical establishment so that the lipid hypothesis became accepted as fact.

But surely doctors would see through that legerdemain, I thought.

Just then I came across an issue of the *British Medical Journal* in January 2003 alleging that, in 1997, a cohort of researchers in Boston with close ties to big pharmaceutical firms ("pharmas") invented the category now called "female sexual dysfunction" — just to push up the sales of Viagra-type drugs.

In recent history, new hard-to-put-your-finger-on diagnoses seem to have passed effortlessly into the lexicon. These include gems like male menopause, attention deficit disorder, advanced sleep phase disorder, even generalised anxiety disorder (GAD), and social anxiety disorder (SAD).

Times were when GAD would just have meant being overly worried, and SAD being a little shy. But not to fret — the antidepressant Prozac, worldwide sales of which rose ten times in the 1990s, can take care of such problems.

These stories would be funny if they weren't so serious.

They highlight two issues.

First, the practice of medicine including clinical research has become conflicted by monied interests.

Conflicts of interest arise when pharmas threaten implicitly to cut off research funding if unfavourable results about their products are reported, or when physicians do trials on products put out by companies they have equity in.

An international study of 789 articles in medical journals found that one-third of authors had a financial interest in the matter they were studying.

Such conflicts could have tragic consequences.

In 1999, Mr Jesse Gelsinger, who was born without a gene needed for processing nitrogen in food proteins, became the first death directly related to gene therapy.

In a trial at the University of Pennsylvania, a virus containing the missing gene was injected into his liver which caused all organs to fail. Mr Gelsinger, who had survived on a careful diet for 18 years, died three days later.

It was later revealed that his physicians and the university had pecuniary interests in the trial. In fact, one doctor held 30 per cent equity — later sold for US$13 million (S$22.6 million) — in the firm that supplied the virus.

In an International Committee of Medical Journal Editors study of 800 life science faculty members, 47 per cent were found to consult for pharmas, 25 per cent had pharma grants, and 8 per cent owned stocks in their pharma sponsors.

With cross-linkages so rampant, doctors will find it easier to balance their Hippocratic with their fiduciary duties only if the law requires full disclosure of their financial interests, if any.

A second issue concerns the often unquestioning acceptance of new fangled diagnoses by doctors, probably because of the sheer overload of information in medicine today.

Doctors consistently say that what they gain from medical journals has the greatest impact on their practice. Even if true, this confidence may be unjustified because journals frequently include anecdotal case reports but the time-pressed doctor may fail to read about systematic studies done subsequently that disconfirm such reports.

There are 25,000 biomedical journals worldwide, or two million articles annually. Medline, the electronic database with 10 million citations, adds 30,000 new references monthly, yet covers only 4,000 journals.

Little wonder many doctors cannot keep up and are, in fact, inordinately influenced by industry advertising whether through print media, symposia sponsorship, or a visit by a sales representative when exaggerated claims are not unusual.

This would be of no concern if doctors routinely discounted such information but research indicates that advertising does influence prescribing behaviour — even if most doctors say that being wined and dined by pharmas does not.

There is no solution but for practitioners to track down the best evidence with which to answer clinical questions.

Continuing medical education already required in some Asian jurisdictions may impel the time-pressed practitioner to get up-to-speed more efficiently so patients can trust what they say again.

On my part, I did not start on statins.

Taking statins to be safe? You may be sorry

HAVE you had your statin this morning? That's a pill you take if you have a cholesterol level so high that dieting won't bring it down. Millions around the world are popping these pills, which are billion-dollar best-sellers for their manufacturers.

Excess cholesterol causes gunk to build up in the walls of arteries, narrowing the bore, thus blocking them. Blockages may result in heart attacks or strokes, while statins lower cholesterol levels, thus preventing such blockages.

Some are now proposing that people with what have been called normal cholesterol levels take statins for life.

Is this idea sound?

Up until now, it has been accepted wisdom that people with too much bad cholesterol (low-density lipoprotein or LDL) should receive statins — unless they also have high levels of good cholesterol (high-density lipoprotein or HDL). Both LDL and HDL are actually proteins that transport cholesterol, albeit in opposite directions: LDL trucks cholesterol to heart and brain arteries, where it is laid down to form gunk. HDL shovels cholesterol away from these arteries, ferrying the artery clogger to the liver for processing.

However, recent studies, like one published in the *Journal Of The American Medical Association* in March 2004, claim that your good cholesterol may be of a malfunctioning variety.

Depending on your genes, your HDL may not actually be protecting your heart. But we can't tell for sure since the blood test gives you only your total cholesterol level, not its functionality. Just to be safe, proponents reason, why not take statins even if you have lots of so-called "good cholesterol"?

But the track record of statins gives cause for pause.

Introduced in 1987, they are the most potent of cholesterol-lowering agents — but hardly the safest. For example, a particular statin called Baycol (cerivastatin) was withdrawn in 2001 after apparently causing 1,100 cases of muscle weakness and at least 100 fatalities.

Though statins, as a class of drugs, have been around for more than 16 years, no study of any particular statin exceeds four years. It is fair to say, therefore, that what its side effects might be after you have been popping one for 20 years make for a huge unknown.

What is already well known but widely understated is that statin-poppers could develop muscle and memory problems.

First, statins carry a small but definite risk of causing potentially fatal muscle problems as they can cause a toxic reaction leading to what is called rhabdomyolysis. The patient develops severe muscle aches, soreness or weakness — and brown urine, perhaps the most tell-tale symptom.

Initially described with crush injuries suffered in the World War II bombing blitz of London, rhabdomyolysis means that muscles are disintegrating and pouring out toxic muscle cell components into the bloodstream. These toxic products then sneak through the meshwork of kidney capillaries to clog up the fine urine-forming tubes. The end result is kidney failure.

Rhabdomyolysis, which accounted for all the Baycol deaths, may be caused by any statin currently on the market. The risk: One death for every million of statin prescriptions. So if you are on one and have some muscle pain or weakness for no obvious reason, you should not let your doctor tell you to take an aspirin and call him in the morning.

There is a second reason for doctors to take their patients' complaints of vague pains seriously: Statins may also cause cognitive problems.

It is now known that lowered cholesterol levels tend to be associated with low serotonin levels, the chemical in the brain that modulates mood, emotion, sleep and appetite. One particular side effect that is attracting attention is aggressive or violent behaviour in some when their cholesterol levels nosedive.

While it is true that published statin studies don't even hint at such a link, it is equally true they were not designed to elucidate such a connection. A random, double-blind trial (which prevents doctor and patient bias) now under way at the University of California in San Diego will help sort this out. It was reported in the journal *Archives Of Internal Medicine* in February 2004 and the results are due out in 2005.

Statins may cause other side effects as well, such as raising liver enzymes, the significance of which is unclear.

So, should healthy people with normal cholesterol levels take statins preventively as proponents suggest?

Probably not, if some University of British Columbia analyses are anything to go by. Pooling data from seven best statin trials carried out on people with high cholesterol and coronary disease, the Canadian investigators found that (secondary) preventive usage of statins did stave off a second catastrophic event and reduced fatality rates.

In parallel analyses of five best statin trials carried out on people with high cholesterol but no coronary disease, they found that (primary) preventive usage was quite futile. They reported in *Therapeutic Letter* in September 2003 that only one in 70 such people put on statins are saved from a heart attack or stroke. Even then, fatality rates are not reduced. Extrapolating, it makes sense that if your cholesterol levels have always been normal and your ticker is healthy, taking statins preventively would probably not benefit anyone.

Except drug firms.

Recent events make such a sceptical attitude seem very wise.

The latest American standards for treating high cholesterol levels which are usually adopted by doctors in Asia, issued in July 2004, lowered the threshold for considering the aggressive use of the expensive drugs called statins. For people already afflicted with coronary heart disease, but have low LDL levels between 70 and 100, the US National Institutes of Health (NIH) now recommends using statins to lower LDL to under 70.

This will not be an easy goal because while a standard dose of statins gets most people close to 100, you will need very high doses to get down to 70, if ever. When you consider that doubling a statin dose lowers LDL levels by another 6 per cent only, getting to 70 might take near-toxic doses.

Lower thresholds were also proposed for millions of women and elderly people at moderately high risk of heart disease, as well as diabetics. These are people who have not developed coronary heart disease yet but do have risk factors, like older age, hypertension or smoking, which can increase one's risk of a heart attack in the next decade by 10 to 20 per cent.

Previously, doctors would prescribe statins to this group only if LDL surpassed 130. They were also deemed to have reached good levels anytime their LDL dropped below 130.

But now NIH urges that more statins be used in this group to bring LDL levels below 100, so people who were told that their LDL levels were good enough when the authorities revised their recommendations in 2001 are being told this year that they aren't low enough.

In much of Asia, the acceptable LDL level for this group at moderate risk is still 130. If we follow the new US guidelines, we'll have to put many, many people on statins — and that may not be supported by the evidence available.

Here's why.

When the NIH recommendations were initially published in the journal, *Circulation*, the fact that eight of the nine authors had received research grants or consultancy fees from statin makers was not disclosed. In medicine, such disclosure is now par for the course.

When the authors were queried, they did not deny the financial links but claimed that the non-disclosure was a mere oversight. Granted, their very stature meant that they were also the very people whose advice industry would seek but panelists who write public health guidelines must assure the public that they are not swayed by drug companies that can benefit from their recommendations.

After all, really big bucks are involved: In 2004, the world market for cholesterol drugs was worth more than US$25 billion, with statins accounting for 90 per cent of that market.

So we should be sceptical.

Does the evidence cited by NIH to justify the new guidelines pass muster?

It doesn't.

Thus argues a group of more than three dozen doctors, scientists and epidemiologists from universities like Harvard and Stanford who, in September 2004, petitioned the NIH to convene an independent panel to review the report. They showed that the studies NIH cited do not prove that statins benefit women of any age, or men over 70 who do not already have heart disease, while three of the four studies of diabetics show no significant benefit. Furthermore, one of the five cited studies shows that statins increase the risk of cancer in the elderly.

What to do?

Clearly, these new guidelines should not be indiscriminately applied to all segments of the population, so doctors in Asia must keep their own counsel on this.

Be sure to ask your doctor if he does.

"Pre-disease" — Has medicine gone mad?

IMAGINE how absurd it would be for doctors to call healthy people "pre-diseased". Well, in August 2003, the latest set of guidelines issued in the United States on the treatment of high blood pressure brandished a new term: "Pre-hypertension".

While unlikely that they will be widely adopted, the new guidelines make the controversial recommendation that doctors tell people with blood pressures between 120/80 and 140/90 mm Hg that they are "pre-hypertensive".

No doctor would quibble that anyone with a blood pressure of more than 140/90 is hypertensive and would require medication to keep it under control, that otherwise he runs the higher risk of getting a stroke or heart attack.

But as to the new guidelines called JNC 7 issued by the US Joint National Committee on Prevention, Detection, Evaluation and Treatment of High Blood Pressure, many doctors will need to be convinced.

In blood pressure measurements, the upper figure indicates the pressure in the blood vessels during that split-second when the heart is pumping out blood. The lower figure is the pressure in vessels when the heart is resting between contractions.

With the latest recommendation, untold numbers may be labelled pre-hypertensive — and be put on medication they may not need, simply because they are "pre-something".

How did it come to this?

Using a statistical manipulation of data from 30 major clinical trials done on hypertension treatment that did not start out measuring the same things, JNC 7 concluded that the risk of heart attack and stroke from hypertension begins at 115/75 — not 140/90 as had been accepted for a long time almost everywhere.

If nothing else, the notion of being "pre-hypertensive" will create anxiety, when not everyone so labelled will get a heart attack or stroke.

What the guidelines allow for, is that the prehypertensive person will be told, in the first instance, to lose weight, avoid sodium-rich foods, exercise regularly, stop smoking and reduce stress. While these are sensible habits, they are not likely to reduce one's blood pressure by much. So it may not be far down the road when medication is prescribed — for life.

A wiser approach than the US guidelines is perhaps the one taken by the European Society of Hypertension and the European Society of Cardiology, whose guidelines do not fixate on a number but recommend that doctors treat hypertension on the basis of a patient's overall risk.

That is, customise the therapy.

For example, a patient with a reading of 132/84 but no other illness may not need treatment. However, a patient with a lower reading of, say, 122/82 who has diabetes, or a father or mother who died from a heart attack or stroke, should probably be on anti-hypertensive drugs.

While guidelines deal with diseases, doctors deal with patients, each presenting different situations.

The common practice is to have people with high readings — but none of the changes that hypertension typically causes in the eyes or kidneys — lie down and relax in a quiet room for 20 minutes. Measurements are then re-taken, which would invariably be lower and normal, as emotional stress, smoking, caffeine, decongestants, a cold room or a full bladder can all give false high readings.

Unfortunately, under pressure of time, doctors may choose to medicate instead of doing all this to rule out a false positive.

If your doctor says you are pre-hypertensive, or hypertensive, observe if he does all of the following to confirm the diagnosis.

First, your readings must be taken with your arm supported at the level of your heart — and only after you have been seated for at least five minutes. Second, if the pressure is high, he should retake it after five minutes with you lying down and immediately when you stand up. It should also be taken again two minutes later.

These steps are to make sure that raised readings are not just due to your heart and blood systems rebalancing when your body changes positions.

Third, he should take at least two readings at each visit with as big an interval between the two as possible.

Finally, he should have three sets of high readings that are at least one week apart before he recommends starting you on drugs for life.

While sticks and stones may break some bones, words can also hurt.

As the title of anti-Fascism author Carlo Levi's 1955 work *Le Parole Sono Pietre* states: "Words are stones".

So don't take it lying down if your doctor says you are pre-hypertensive.

Your liver enzymes look high?

FOLLOWING that act of brutal intimacy called the annual medical with its obligatory digital examination of the rectum, your doctor rhapsodises about your health. Then he drops that clanger: "Except that your liver enzymes look somewhat high".

He doesn't quite explain, but these enzymes are protein catalysts residing inside your liver cells. They enable the organ to process fats, sugars and proteins, then get rid of the waste products that result.

When liver cells are injured, enzymes called AST (aspartate aminotransferase) and ALT (alanine aminotransferase), gush out with a vengeance. Thus when your raised enzyme levels — or raised enzymes — are of these types, they may indicate some liver injury.

But how much is too much?

Normally, there are about five to 50 units of either in each liter of blood. The accepted healthy threshold is 50. But in practice, any reading ranging from 100 to 200 or even 300 may be seen in apparently healthy people. These readings could mean liver problems — or they may not. Even when there is actual liver damage, enzyme levels don't correlate with the degree of damage. An AST of 300 does not mean twice as bad as 150.

In addition, not every liver disease produces raised enzymes. In some people with advanced liver diseases, their enzyme levels are normal. That is why it's difficult for your doctor to give a precise explanation for what's going on in your body.

What a high enzyme reading means in an individual depends on his specific medical condition. One reading alone, especially when taken during an annual medical, doesn't give doctors much of a clue, as most people go for their annuals only when they feel well. With little to work on, doctors can only adopt a wait-and-see attitude.

Meanwhile, they will check that you haven't contracted hepatitis B or C from unprotected sex, through blood transfusions or intravenous drug abuse; that you have not been using various herbs and cholesterol-lowering drugs or aspirin; and that there is no history of liver disease in your family.

If the answer to all these is "no", they will conclude that nothing seems amiss despite your high enzyme reading.

So you're home free?

Not quite.

In the early 1990s, doctors identified a condition that causes raised liver enzymes in the apparently healthy. In ducks and geese, it would be called *foie gras,* that gourmet appetiser consisting of the liver of waterfowl that has been force-fed corn over three weeks to bulk the organ up with fat. In humans, the condition is now called non-alcoholic fatty liver, to differentiate it from the fatty liver that alcoholics frequently develop. In this condition, an excess of the hormone called insulin blocks the liver from burning off fats called triglycerides inside its cells.

Triglycerides thus accumulate in them to balloon them up.

These triglycerides are toxic to liver cells, causing inflammation (hepatitis) and provoking the liver to lay down collagen. That's the stuff doctors inject into the face to smoothen wrinkles out, but this collagen is abnormal and stimulates the organ to develop scars (cirrhosis).

So it is just like *foie gras*?

Compared to how quickly *foie gras* is produced, however, this fattening of the human liver is an indolent process. Although first identified in 1980, it was smouldering so slowly that doctors took fatty liver to be an innocuous condition. They would take another decade to observe the inflammation and scarring that was setting in at a snail's pace.

Now the $64 question: How likely is it that your raised enzymes might indicate a fatty liver?

The diagnosis can only be confirmed with a liver biopsy, but fatty liver is very likely — about 88 per cent chance in one study — if you are also obese, afflicted with diabetes, and have raised fat levels as well.

But there's a 60 per cent chance that your fatty liver, if you have one, will remain quiescent and harmless. However, there is also a 40 per cent chance that it might go on to develop hepatitis, then fatal scarring, the condition called liver cirrhosis.

So help yourself.

Avoid those so-called liver tonics as none have been backed up by credible studies. Even worse are those herbs that may hurt the liver, like germander which Western herbalists use for weight loss, and *shou wu* which Chinese herbalists use for prematurely greying hair.

You may want to take lots of soya products. A soya bean extract called PPC (polyenylphosphatidylcholine), already approved in Europe for use in chronic liver diseases, may reverse this disease process.

Finally, lay off extremely rich foods, lose some weight, treat that diabetes and lower those blood fats.

Do we really need full annual health checks?

IN the third century BC, the ruthless emperor who first unified all of China, Shi Huangdi, admonished: "The superior physician helps before the early budding of the disease, not when it is already in full bloom".

Modern doctors and their ever hopeful patients think they can go even further and keep most illnesses from occurring in the first place — by an annual physical examination.

It has become a ritual for many, especially if you are an executive and your employer foots the bill.

In September 2003, the US Agency for Healthcare Research and Quality (AHRQ) concluded after a series of studies that began 14 years earlier that such regular check-ups do not extend life or decrease illnesses or discomfort.

The agency said that listening to hearts, thumping chests, looking at the eyes, ears and throats of healthy individuals — and the uncomfortable parts when the doctor probes one's rectum and vagina, or feels one's testes, as the case may be — do not improve survival rates.

The routine annual chest X-rays, electrocardiograms (ECGs), urine analysis and blood work, it concluded, are also unnecessary. Indeed, what many consider a cornerstone of preventive health care has, for a long while, been an unproven notion in Western medicine.

How then did it come about?

Its genesis may be traced to a 1919 report by an American insurer, Metropolitan Life Insurance, that people who had annual physicals also died later in life.

But this was putting the cart before the horse: You had an annual physical only if you were healthy, so whenever an older individual had one, he was both disease-free and alive!

Still, the medical fraternity swallowed the flawed logic and began advising healthy people to see their doctors for a head-to-toe physical exam, which came with a battery of tests and a conference to discuss the results. In 1947, the American Medical Association formalised that recommendation for everyone over 35.

This idea lay unexamined until 1979, when the Canadian government set up a task force on "the periodic health examination".

Its conclusions: The annual physical was quite unnecessary. Whatever the health advice proffered at the annual, it could also be doled out in small doses during visits for other reasons.

In 1984, the US government set up a similar task force which came largely to the same conclusion. It surmised that only a full medical history to identify health risk factors, and measurements of height, weight and blood pressure were of any proven worth in symptom-free people. Blood work, urine analysis and ECGs were more money than they were worth.

Yet the medical establishment continued to recommend a check-up once every five years for people under 40, and once every one to three years thereafter.

As the evidence mounted, even this could not be maintained. The latest AHRQ study says, in fact, that annual physicals frequently result in false positives — that is, false alarms.

These, in turn, lead to unnecessary tests.

But a lot of healthy people do go for physicals simply because they think they are supposed to. In fact, the more exams and tests done, the better patients feel about themselves and their doctors.

The reason? Patients are unaware that there is little evidence that the annual physical significantly improves one's health. In fact, physicians who try to advise their patients that this is the case, risk having them go away dissatisfied.

What's a doctor to do?

Older practitioners who have been doing annuals out of habit tend to protest that the absence of evidence is not evidence of uselessness. They say that, if nothing, the annual carves out a time to offer lifestyle and nutritional advice. They also claim that it helps maintain an inner sense of well being for the patient, and fosters trust and confidence in the doctor.

But there is little evidence this is true.

Doctors generally try to make the time to fit preventive advice, screening tests and vaccinations into other visits that their patients make for minor problems.

What's a patient to do?

Economists call relationships between doctor and patient, or lawyer and litigant, and so on, one of "informational asymmetry". That is, a lot of relevant information is known to the doctor or the lawyer, but not the client.

To right this imbalance somewhat, the patient must build his own knowledge base — for example, by using health information which is freely available online.

He should strive to understand the major health risks at his current age, how to prevent them, and what the age-appropriate tests are.

For example, screening for colorectal and breast cancers after 50 is worth the effort. ECGs may be wise even earlier, if a close relative had a heart attack at a relatively young age, for example.

So don't burn all your bridges with the health-screeners.

The doctor is not a high priest just because he lays the stethoscope on your chest, but someone you can discuss these things with. Since the jury is in on the annual physical, work out with your doctor, instead, on the specific screening tests you really need and when you need them.

Ruthlessly decline everything else.

Don't ignore that frequent heartburn

YOU gorge on extra-spicy chilli crab at dinner. Then you stuff your face with pepperoni pizza just before retiring. You get heartburn afterwards, a burning sensation in the chest behind the breastbone. There might also be a sour taste in the mouth.

If this happens ever so often, you might have Gerd, or gastroesophageal reflux disease.

Reflux occurs when the stomach's contents flow back up into the oesophagus, a muscular tube that carries food from throat to stomach. The stomach's highly acidic contents can go all the way up to the voice box (larynx), into the back of the mouth and nose. In the process, the delicate membranes lining the insides of the oesophagus and larynx may be inflamed and damaged.

But why does food go the wrong way? There's a special ring of muscle called a sphincter that surrounds the lowermost end of the oesophagus where it joins the stomach. Acting like a gate, it relaxes to let food in at the right time, then tightens up to prevent food from going back up the wrong way.

Should it open indiscriminately, however, acidic liquid stomach content (refluxate) then sloshes up the oesophagus.

Actually, reflux happens to most of us in our waking hours. In the upright position, however, the refluxate flows back down under gravity. Also, unawares, we're frequently swallowing our saliva, which helps wash any refluxate down. In addition, saliva contains bicarbonate that neutralises any acid left in the oesophagus. Chewing gum stimulates saliva production and makes us swallow more often, so gum after a meal does more than freshen your breath.

When reclining, however, there is no swallowing or gravitational pull. Also, we secrete less saliva while asleep. So nocturnal reflux is likely to see acid remain longer and damage the oesophagus.

The occasional overindulgence in food and drink may cause some reflux without permanent damage. But in those who develop Gerd, the refluxate often contains more acid and remains longer in the oesophagus. The reason lies in a lax sphincter — excessive alcohol and tobacco use renders it lax — that contracts too weakly or relaxes at the wrong time and stays relaxed too long.

Gerd is usually treated with gastric ulcer medication to decrease the stomach's acid production. Sometimes, surgery may be necessary.

If unsatisfactorily treated, and after years of exposure to acid, the membrane lining the oesophagus may become pre-cancerous. With the membrane desensitised to acid, there may be fewer symptoms to warn the patient and a fatal cancer may result. In fact, Gerd has been in the news lately precisely because of this link: In the United States, it is now noted that this very deadly cancer has increased fivefold in 30 years.

How to prevent the cancer? One way is to screen for pre-cancer with endoscopy, where a thin, fibre-optic lighted tube is lowered down the throat to look at the oesophagus and take biopsy samples. Although uncomfortable, it takes only 30 minutes to complete.

Whom to screen remains an unanswered question. After all, Gerd is said to be less frequent in Asians because the generally smaller bodies produce less acid. But, as Associate Professor Ho Khek Yu of the National University Hospital was the first to observe, lower Asian rates arise also because Chinese, Malay and Tamil languages have no word for heartburn. So older patients can't report it cogently to their physicians who, unsurprisingly, seldom endoscope them.

"Our patients are reporting it better in English now", said Prof Ho who, in 1994, showed that only 2 per cent of Asian adults in Singapore had heartburn more than once a month. In his recent re-survey of the same community, he showed a four-fold increase. An increase in actual erosive damage (oesophagitis) was also noted on endoscopy.

Recent studies from Taiwan also report oesophagitis in 15 per cent; Hong Kong just reported a 10 per cent incidence of Gerd. Professor Ho notes "Gerd is rapidly increasing in prevalence in different parts of Asia". Perhaps it's time to screen people who have frequent heartburn? While an *Archives of Internal Medicine* review of the best studies in July 2003 surmised that screening was worthwhile, the journal *Gastroenterology* reported that a panel of experts it had convened was of the consensus that screening wasn't cost effective. In other words, it's good to screen if money is no object.

On a separate note for folk with kids: Reflux is an under-appreciated and overlooked problem in childhood because kids don't complain of heartburn. Instead, they may have repeated coughing, frequent vomiting, poor weight gain, discomfort in swallowing, or fretfulness after a meal. Or tiny tots could simply present sleepless nights — writhing and crying incessantly but quieting down when carried upright. If you have a "colicky" child, you might want to ask your pediatrician about Gerd.

Neurolinguistic programming and brainwashing

IN many Asian countries, there are many neurolinguistic programming (NLP) trainers who make a good living helping students analyse their learning styles and "reprogramming" their brains.

Proponents say "neuro" in NLP refers to the nerve cells or working units of the nervous system which send, receive and process signals that become information; "linguistic" refers to the signals moving across these networks; and "programming" is about manipulating the content of those signals into useful information.

What do these NLP practitioners actually do?

They say they help people change by teaching them to reprogramme their brains. Two metaphors repeatedly used liken NLP to a user's manual, or software, for the brain. What is stressed is a variety of communication and persuasion skills, as well as self-hypnosis. Like any New Age therapy, it promises a painless way to become more creative, intelligent, healthy, rich and fulfilled.

All that for the price of admission.

In Singapore, a basic seven-day course costs US$1,500. You can next move on to a master practitioner course lasting 14 days, and then be certified to train others if you complete the 21-day trainer course thereafter.

Dozens of individuals are subjected together to days of intense instruction on how to unearth their personal obstacles to a fulfilling life. There is much ado about observing behaviour and learning to read "body language".

At some level, NLP must assume that the same things hinder everyone, since its one approach suits all.

Perhaps that is why, unlike psychotherapists, its practitioners don't scour around for a problem's roots. Instead, they focus on how to solve it, which they do by homing in on, not psychology, but communication — verbal language, body language and eye movements.

Its basic premise is that how people express themselves outwardly reveals how they perceive and represent their problems internally and subconsciously. That internal representation can supposedly involve any of the five senses, and purportedly is reflected in one's choice of words, tone of voice, eye movements, breathing patterns and body posture.

For example, someone in a visual mode may say, "I see a way to . . .", while a person who has stored auditory images could say, "That sounds about right to me". An individual in the kinesthetic mode may say, "I feel that . . .", but if I squeeze my nose while talking to you, it may mean I think your idea stinks. Of course, in the gustatory mode, I'd say, "I taste victory".

And so on.

The NLP therapist analyses your phraseology, scrutinises your facial expressions, and observes your body language. In this way, he says, he ascertains your internal state of, say, apprehension, happiness, and so on. Next, he helps you remodel your thoughts to overcome the negative mental associations that are hindering you from achieving your full potential. This is by substituting positive thinking patterns in their place. Fans believe that successful people have certain patterns of thinking — so recognising these patterns are fundamental — and the brain can be taught these patterns to bring about self-improvement.

This is why NLP is said to be about modelling human excellence. The claim is that its experts have studied the thinking and behaviour patterns of successful people and then extracted models of how they work, which lesser mortals can use.

But how do we know which model, if any, is correct?

Asked for scientific proof, practitioners tend to argue that it is difficult to prove anything that has to do with the mind. Most practitioners admit NLP is not a science, which is why they don't have to offer scientific proof.

The small body of scientific research done by others on NLP shows no correlation between eye movements and reported thoughts, or word choices, for example. Its presupposition that people can be influenced by appealing directly to the subconscious hasn't been substantiated too.

That is not to say that NLP techniques don't work. In fact, NLP itself declares that what matters is whether it works.

But what does that mean and how do you ascertain if it does work?

It seems to mean one thing: Satisfied customers who feel better or people who think NLP explains their problems to their satisfaction. Practitioners say that the proof NLP works is people keep coming back for more.

Yet this may just reflect how successful trainers have been in convincing customers to re-enrol and/or persuade friends and family to sign up too. There are no objective criteria to determine what is "successful" training, so we also can't be sure who, conversely, hasn't benefited from it. Personal anecdotes and testimonies, the main signposts of success in NLP, are no substitutes for scientific studies under controlled conditions to ensure people aren't deceiving themselves.

Like being brainwashed?

Practitioners typically agree that NLP is about manipulating the behaviour of others — but one can't avoid manipulating people anyway, they insist. With NLP training, at least, you know you are doing it, and you decide what beliefs to "install", they rationalise.

They call it reprogramming but some NLP trainers are not unhappy to call it brainwashing people — because they say it is for the better.

And make a good living while helping others?

Great job if you can get it.

V. What's that in my food?

Eat French fries at your own risk ...

FISH and chips is quintessentially English, but even the most ardent Anglophile can't deny that those chips are soggy and messy. On the other hand, the golden deep-fried chips Americans call French fries are quite another story: You don't have to wash your hands after you have had them, renamed freedom fries after the Iraq war.

In fact, McDonald's and Burger King have patented ways of frying their fries so hot they come out really dry and crispy. Scientists now say, however, that the hotter and drier they are fried, the more they have acrylamide, a chemical ordinarily used to purify sewage.

In April 2002, Swedish scientists discovered that some people who hadn't been exposed occupationally to acrylamide but who ate a lot of fries and crispies had blood levels of acrylamide higher than those the World Health Organisation (WHO) recommends for drinking water.

Many countries have since confirmed those findings.

Because acrylamide causes cancer in rodents, eating fries and crispies may put you at risk. And while Asians may not consume the 15 kg of fries an average American does each year, we're probably not too far behind. Then there are local dishes whose acrylamide content we don't know about yet.

There is, in fact, research on Asian food that the Health Sciences Authority in Singapore does for industry clients, for example, but they won't divulge their findings. However, there is a study of 400 Hong Kong food items published in the journal called *Food Additives And Contaminants* in December 2003 showing that potato-based products have the most acrylamide, while rye-, corn-, wheat- and rice-based products have progressively lower levels, in that order.

The researchers also found that frying yew char kway (wheat-based dough fritters) longer and hotter led to more acrylamide being formed. Chinese rice crispies, however, had the lowest levels of the chemical. Meanwhile, when issuing its action plan in late March 2004 that seeks to reduce the potential risk of acrylamide in food, the United States Food and Drug Administration (FDA) released a new batch of results on American food. The list showed that while KFC, McDonald's and Burger King French fries as well as Frito Lay crispies were chockful of it, Pringles crispies took top prize with five to ten times more. However, KFC mashed potato had very little acrylamide.

So you now know what to avoid.

Or do you?

Truth be told, acrylamide is very widespread in the entire food supply.

So, while gingerbread contains high levels, naan bread, crumpets and fruitcake contain much less than other bread products. Acrylamide is also found in bottled prune juice, black olives, asparagus and almonds as well as fried chicken and fast-food chicken nuggets. And so on.

Here's the skinny on it all: While a few foods contribute most to one's total daily acrylamide exposure, no single food contributes a majority. Besides varying widely from food to food, acrylamide levels also vary from brand to brand of the same food, even from lot to lot of the same brand. What's a consumer to avoid?

The best rule of thumb, at least for the moment: Crust.

Brown crust forms on breads, pastries, biscuits and fries when proteins are transformed in the presence of sugars. This happens fastest at high temperatures and also leads to acrylamide formation.

Specifically, it is foods rich in asparagine (a major amino acid in potatoes and cereals) and glucose that can form a lot of acrylamide, especially when cooked above 120 deg C as in frying, grilling, roasting or baking. When moisture is present, as in boiling, however, acrylamide doesn't form.

Of course, all this matters only if acrylamide is a clear and present danger to humans. True, it is widely accepted to be a rodent carcinogen, but extrapolating this to humans is not a done deal.

For one thing, cancers in laboratory rats are induced by doses several times higher than what we ingest in our daily meals: A 70 kg person must consume 80 kg of French fries, or 140 kg of Cheerios cereals, every day — for life — to approach the lowest risk levels observed in lab rats.

For another thing, human metabolism differs from rats. In 1977, the US authorities proposed to ban saccharin after it was found to cause cancer in rats. In fact, that applied to only male rats because they have a unique biochemical process to metabolise saccharin, something female rats — and humans — don't possess.

So does this rat carcinogen really cause cancers in humans?

To rule this out, big population studies are needed to ascertain if people with high acrylamide intake also have higher cancer rates. One small study published in the *British Journal Of Cancer* in January 2003 found no such link with bladder, colon or kidney cancers in people. (In rats, however, acrylamide causes cancers of the lung, testes, breast and uterus.)

In March 2003, a small Italian study published in the *International Journal Of Cancer* concluded likewise. Yet, such studies of only a few hundred cases may not be sensitive enough to detect any link, if it exists, given that acrylamide is estimated to cause fewer than 1 per cent of all cancers. As these studies remain inconclusive, scientists await the results of the FDA and WHO's ongoing larger-scale studies.

At this point, we simply don't know what the actual health risk the acrylamide found in our food poses. Still, one thing is clear. There has long been good reason to eat less of greasy French fries and snack crispies.

In the meantime, acrylamide may be one more reason to eat even less of them.

Palm oil bad? Get those fat facts right

IF you are vacationing in Malaysia and you are driving from Singapore up the North-South Highway which spans the peninsula, in under an hour from the Lion City, vast expanses of dark and dank oil palm estates begin to greet you on your left. As you cruise on, closely planted palm trees seem to cover the landscape without a break.

This is the plant whose fruit gives an edible oil that is sold in bulk to Singapore, which repackages it for export worldwide.

Palm oil, however, tends to be stigmatised as a saturated oil that can only drive up bad cholesterol, which plasters thick layers inside your arteries. (Good cholesterol, by contrast, chips away at the gunk and trucks it off.)

Saturated oil's unsavoury reputation comes from the oft-repeated idea that all saturated fats drive up bad cholesterol, while unsaturated fats decrease the artery clogger in your blood. It is an old saw that palm oil is bad for you because it raises your cholesterol.

But this idea needs some nuancing.

Consider this.

First, the oil palm fruit produces two different oils. It has an edible outer, fleshy pulp, or mesocarp; a middle layer of inedible shell; and an innermost layer of edible kernel, or endosperm. The distinctively red cooking oil you can grab off supermarket shelves here comes from the pulp, not the kernel. (The red colour is due to the same compound found in tomatoes called carotenoids, or vitamin A.)

On the other hand, the kernel inside the hard shell gives a more expensive light yellow oil which you couldn't buy if you tried: It's only marketed industrially to makers of cocoa butter substitutes, non-dairy creamers, soaps, and so on. The point to note is that the same fruit produces two different oils, each with different types of fats, in different proportions of saturated and unsaturated fats.

The pulp oil is uniquely half-and-half, or 50 per cent saturated and 50 per cent unsaturated; the latter, specifically, being 40 per cent mono-unsaturated fats, and 10 per cent poly-unsaturated fats. (The former will, while the latter may, reduce bad cholesterol.)

By contrast, palm kernel oil is 86-12-02 in that order, much like coconut (kernel) oil, which is 92-06-02. To be sure, costly olive oil wins at 14-77-09, while inexpensive peanut oil is a graceful 18-49-33.

Yet, raw numbers don't always tell the whole story.

Thus, secondly, however provocative these vital statistics may be, the human body doesn't treat all consumed fats the same. Apparently, some saturated fats we eat raise one's level of bad cholesterol more than others.

Why is this so?

Truth be told, this isn't something completely understood yet. However, it is thought that different saturated fats differ in their effects on those docking stations in human cells where bad cholesterol must lodge before it can begin its dastardly work.

Ingested saturated fats may also differ in their individual effects on the many enzymes the body uses to process fats. They may also affect how fast both bad and good cholesterol get transported around the body.

Finally, besides ingested fats, the liver makes a lot of cholesterol every day which the body uses to make the hormones we need. However, palm oil has lots of one form of vitamin E called tocotrienol, a super-antioxidant that discourages the liver from doing too much of that. So palm oil reduces the body's own production of cholesterol as well. For all these reasons, though it may well be 50 per cent saturated, palm oil does not increase bad cholesterol.

This has also been documented in many trials, each standing up to international standards of clinical testing and published in respectable journals, and covering different populations — in the Netherlands, Australia, China, Pakistan, India and Malaysia.

True, older studies in the 1970s showed opposite results, but these were carried out with excessively high fat diets on old subjects already afflicted with elevated levels of cholesterol. The newer studies were done without these biases.

University of Pennsylvania expert David Kritchevsky, in an overview for a symposium published in the Singapore-based *Asia-Pacific Journal of Clinical Nutrition* in 2002, concluded that "palm oil is a safe, wholesome and nutritious edible oil".

Even if you disagree with that, the take-home lesson here, at the very least, is this: Experts are convinced that saturated fats are not all equal. The rest of us need to learn which ones are bad for us — and which good.

Or, know your fat facts.

Watch that margarine

OREOS, those gorgeous cookies that every child loves, contain trans fatty acids, also called trans fats. These are so bad for health that Kraft Foods, the largest food-maker in the United States, is promising to eliminate them from next year.

The giant American snack company Frito-Lay, which said its popular Doritos, Tostitos and Cheetos chips will be free of trans fats by September, became the first major company to voluntarily reveal trans fat content on its labels early in 2003.

What is unusual about trans fats, however, is that they come not from animal fats but plant oils that have been hardened by hydrogenation, widely used as margarine and shortening.

The US Food and Drug Administration (FDA) issued a new rule in July 2003 requiring food-makers to list the amount of trans fats in their products.

It could not have come sooner for concerned scientists and consumer activists who have been battling the edible oils industry over this issue since the 1970s.

In 1995, the FDA finally accepted the scientific proof that had been building up inexorably.

Trans fats may well account for a large part of the rise in coronary heart disease over the last century. For instance, the Nurses' Health Study, conducted by Harvard University on 85,000 women since 1976, showed a definite link between trans fats and coronary heart disease.

Non-existent in nature except for minute amounts in the bowels of some ruminants like goats and cows, trans fats are now found in frightening amounts in our diet, an estimated 58 g per day, because consumers have been told for 40 years now that plant oils are better than animal fats, margarine than butter, and so on.

The truth is, the harder a margarine the more trans fat it includes. This synthetic molecule of bad fat also appears in food such as French fries made with "partially hydrogenated vegetable shortening".

Other code words on product labels that hint at the presence of the misfit molecule include the following: Vegetable shortening, partially hydrogenated vegetable oil, or partially hardened cooking oil.

If you look hard enough, you'll see these words on the product labels of cookies, chips, pastries, cakes, breakfast cereals, bottled salad dressings, white bread, even some baby food.

All fats and oils are made up of fatty acids, which are molecules of carbon atoms hooked together like a string of beads that have hydrogen atoms hanging on to the top and bottom of each carbon atom.

There are three main types of fatty acids: saturated, monounsaturated and polyunsaturated.

The "new" menace is a type of saturated fat with a twist, literally. A saturated fatty acid has the maximum possible number of hydrogen atoms attached to every carbon atom: It is saturated with hydrogen. These form long, straight molecules that line up next to each other and pack together neatly as solid fats at room temperature, like animal fat does.

If a hydrogen atom is missing from each of two adjacent carbon atoms in the middle of the molecule, there is now a gap that is not saturated (with hydrogen atoms), so the fatty acid is called "monounsaturated".

The gap kinks the molecule, so these molecules don't pack up neatly but remain liquid at room temperature, like vegetable oils.

Fatty acids with more than one pair of hydrogen atoms missing have more gaps or kinks — "polyunsaturated" — so they remain liquid even in the fridge.

At the turn of the last century, a process using heat in the presence of hydrogen and certain metal catalysts was found to convert natural liquid vegetable oils into solid form like animal fats.

Such partially hydrogenated oils like margarine are stiff enough to make foods like pastry, which previously required lard or tallow.

The hydrogen introduced saturates some gaps, but other gaps merely see the hydrogen atoms rearranged to opposite sides of carbon atoms. The rearrangement converts fatty acids from their natural "cis" form to a "trans" position.

The term "cis" means that hydrogen atoms are on the same side of the unsaturated carbon atoms, while "trans" means they are across.

In nature, fatty acids assume the cis form which is naturally curved like a horseshoe, the shape best suited for the body's physiological processes. By moving a hydrogen atom to the wrong place, the molecule gets bent somewhat out of shape so it no longer fits as nicely but may still be taken up in human metabolism.

Most crucially, trans fats can take part in the making of the cell membrane.

When we consume hydrogenated vegetable oils, our metabolism may insert a trans fat in the cell membrane where a cis fat ought to be.

Because the trans fat is a molecular misfit, the cell membrane gets distorted.

Cell membranes are not passive envelopes. Rather, they actively control the vital biochemical exchanges occurring between the inside and outside of our cells.

With trans molecules in the cell membranes, cells cannot function optimally, and LDL (or bad cholesterol) leaks out from the cell into the blood where its level rises, while HDL (or good cholesterol) moves into the cell so its blood level drops.

In the last century, even as the idea that vegetable oils in any form were better than animal fats became widely popularised, coronary heart disease rose in tandem with the increasing consumption of partially hydrogenated vegetable oils.

Several studies have now convinced food authorities like the FDA that trans fats are not just associated with, but in fact can cause, heart disease.

This is no scare *du jour.*

If Kraft agrees that its Oreos need to lose its trans fat, a globalised world with an Americanised diet would do well to pay close attention.

Having sushi? Hold the salmon

IF you celebrate Chinese New Year in Singapore or Malaysia because you are Chinese or because your Chinese friends have invited you to tag along, chances are you'll have some *yu sheng* or raw fish. Or perhaps, you like sushi. Either way, you are likely to eat some raw salmon, which is increasingly being served at lunch buffet spreads too.

Among the health-conscious and relatively affluent worldwide, salmon is standard fare, because it is believed that eating fish at least twice a week may prevent heart disease and stroke.

Salmon is high in heart-protective oils called omega-3 fatty acids, and low in mercury; tuna, by contrast, while also omega-3 rich, has too much mercury, a toxin found in many types of seafood.

The increased global consumption of salmon in recent years has resulted in a phenomenal growth in farms producing a lot of the fish at prices cheaper than wild salmon.

Maybe, we've got to rethink that salmon fillet, though. In January 2004, the journal, *Science*, published a study which found that farmed salmon contained more contaminants than their cousins in the wild.

The most frightening toxin found was PCB (polychlorinated biphenyl), which is associated with cancers of the liver, biliary tract, intestines and skin. Other toxins included dioxin (Agent Orange) and banned pesticides like toxaphene, dieldrin and DDT, all known or suspected causes of cancer and immuno-suppression.

Salmon from Northern Europe, the world's biggest salmon farmers, were the worst, followed by those from North America and Chile.

How did this fishy business come about?

The answer: Fish chow.

A salmon farm is like a grid of about a dozen net-covered pens in the sea, each a hectare in size. Such a farm produces about 800,000 salmon which can be sold within 18 months.

The high density of the salmon population in these farms means that infections can spread easily. To minimise disease, the stock may be given antibiotics and pesticides.

There is also the colouring pigment used. Wild salmon are pink because they eat a small fish called krill that has astaxanthin, a natural carotenoid pigment. Farmed salmon flesh, however, is grey in its natural state. Those that arrive on supermarket shelves derive their exuberant orange colour from the pigment that is added to fish meal.

Finally there is PCB and the like, which are found in many types of fishes but especially in farmed salmon because of their oily diet — 40 per cent fish meal and 25 per cent fish oil.

The reason for such a diet: Since demand for salmon is so high, supply must rise to meet demand, and the fastest way is to bulk up the salmon. (By way of comparison: Farmed freshwater fish like tilapia and carp are fed a diet with only 1 per cent oil.)

You might think that salmon fat is fine, as it's laden with omega-3 fatty acids, which are supposed to be good for health. But the problem is this: Since PCBs are soluble in oil, not water, they accumulate in the layers of salmon fat. More fat equals more PCBs.

The PCBs themselves originate in the small, open-sea fishes that are used to make fish meal.

Yes, wild salmon are also contaminated with PCBs.

In farming, however, this is magnified manifold.

Small fishes from the Atlantic Ocean and Gulf of Mexico are especially tainted with PCBs. When they are ground up to make food pellets, those toxins get pre-concentrated.

When farm salmon are fed these pellets, oil-soluble PCBs begin to accumulate in the thick fat under the skin. By contrast, leaner, wild salmon accumulate toxins 20 to 30 times less efficiently.

So what are the health-conscious to do, given that you can only get omega-3s by eating fish?

You could eat other cold-water deep sea fish like mackerel or herring.

If you insist on salmon, then trim the fat off before cooking. And don't eat it more than once a month, the *Science* report advises.

If, however, you swear off all fish, rest assured soya bean and flaxseed do contain a fatty acid that the body converts into a usable form of omega-3.

In addition, you could take over-the-counter omega-3 supplements as well. Be advised, however, that their long-term effects have not been studied.

Since these capsules can deliver supernormal doses and since they make the blood less likely to clot, high doses might turn out to be harmful. There's also another consideration: As dietary supplements are unregulated, there is no assurance that their cattle-derived gelatin capsules are not contaminated with mad-cow particles.

So it's a tough decision. If you hold off making it but still want to have *yu sheng* anyway, ask for it to be served with the traditional *sai toh* fish instead. Like most varieties of fish, it does contain some omega-3s, just less.

As in many things, moderation is the best solution.

That steak is mad-cow free? Bull!

DURING the 2003 Christmas season, steak houses worldwide were still serving up prime United States beef when news broke that the first US case of mad-cow disease had been detected and that its meat had already entered the food chain.

That particular animal was called a "downer", American parlance for an animal so ill it can't walk when it reaches the slaughterhouse. Under US rules, downers must be tested for mad-cow disease or bovine spongiform encephalopathy (BSE). But their beef can still be sold after "diseased parts" — brain and spinal cord — are removed.

This was to ensure that no one would get infected eating the beef, then-Agriculture Secretary Ann Veneman averred.

"Muscle cuts of meat have almost no risk... I know of no science to show that you can transmit BSE from muscle cuts of meat," she insisted.

Many people believed her, but how credible is such a claim, really?

Not very.

First, abattoir processes in the US leave a lot to be desired.

Even if brain and spinal cord are eviscerated clean from the carcass, infective particles may have already contaminated the meat when the animal was first stunned unconscious, before being slaughtered. US slaughterhouses stun cows by driving 10 cm-long bolts into their heads at 300 kmh so the resulting concussion is sufficient to knock any animal out.

A rod is then stuck into the stun hole to scramble deeper brain tissues. This is to prevent reflex-kicking by the dead animal when workers bind its hind limbs together.

With or without the scrambling, these stunners can force brain tissue into the bloodstream and meat. In a 1996 experiment, Texas A&M University researchers who applied a chemical marker onto stunner bolts later detected markers within the meat.

After the stunning, workers wield a band saw to cut the carcass up into two halves lengthwise, right through the backbone or spinal column. The sawing, however, can spray tiny particles of spinal cord tissue into the air, which then settle down slowly onto carcasses lying around. In any case, mad cows can have the infective particles in their muscles, albeit in smaller numbers, according to a German study published in May. A Swiss study published last month reports that the particles have also shown up in the muscles of human patients who died from the disease.

Second, infection prevention in the US is grossly inadequate.

BSE is not transmitted from cow to cow but, rather, through the consumption of animal feed contaminated with the particles.

In Britain, feeding cattle on the farm with waste from the slaughterhouse, including infected cow tissue, spread BSE widely in the mid-1980s. After the British authorities banned such feed, the United Kingdom feed industry simply sold its feed overseas. This spread BSE across the European cattle industry. Taking its cue from that debacle, the US rightly imposed a ban on British feed from 1997.

But enforcement was another thing.

About 37 tonnes of "meat or offal unfit for human consumption" and intended for animals was still exported to the US after the ban, according to Britain's 1997 export statistics.

Within the US itself, many feed mills have been violating production rules, including two cattle feed mills near the Washington farm where the first US case was identified last week.

The enforcing agency, the Food and Drug Administration (FDA), is "using inaccurate, incomplete and unreliable data to track and oversee feed ban compliance. (It) has no clear enforcement strategy for dealing with firms that do not obey the feed ban", said a report last year by the investigative arm of the US government, the General Accounting Office. FDA data at its own website show that, up to and including October, about 300 firms had no processes in place to prevent brain and spinal cord tissue from co-mingling with other animal waste, did not label their products properly, and so on. Of these, 173 had distributed prohibited materials to farms. Yet, no action was taken against many of them. Not only has enforcement been shoddy, the US feed ban is also merely a partial one.

Rather than completely ban the feeding of blood, fat, meat and bone meal to livestock, the US ban involves only specified offal such as brain and spinal material. These partial measures failed miserably in Britain to contain the spread of BSE.

The US ban allows calves to be fed a milk formula containing cattle blood plasma as a source of supplementary protein.

However, experiments show that infected cow blood can spread BSE. (There is also one confirmed case in Britain of human BSE being acquired through a blood transfusion.)

Third, BSE surveillance in the US is appalling.

The World Health Organisation's guidelines require BSE testing for every downer cow. Europe and Japan reportedly abide by these rules fully, but the rate of testing in the US is dismally low.

Of the millions of cattle slaughtered in the US each year, there are an estimated 195,000 downers. Yet, last year, for example, only 20,526 downers were BSE-tested.

Moreover, the billion-dollar cattle industry has been able, repeatedly and recently, to block legislation that aims to prevent downer cows from being sold as food. Thus, even a BSE-positive downer can be sold for food as the December 2003 case amply demonstrated.

US beef safe to eat? Sure — if it is organic beef from cows that were not raised on feed but grazed on grass, and slaughtered conscious, not stunned. It just costs a little more. Meanwhile some nations have banned US beef imports. You should also stay away from it when you next visit a steak house in your neighbourhood.

Mad cow disease in that vitamin?

IN 2003, an Australian firm making nutritional supplements sold world wide was found to have seriously breached good manufacturing practices, leading many consumers to fall ill after taking some of its products. The Sydney-based firm called Pan Pharmaceutical which made vitamins, nutritional supplements, herbal concoctions, non-prescription painkillers and cold remedies had hundreds of its products recalled worldwide after it was blacklisted by the Australian authorities.

Pan managers may have cut corners and resorted to unhygienic and unsafe measures in their manufacturing practices since 1998. It is ironic that consumers who resort to "natural" therapies out of fear that Western medicine may harm them could be in trouble after taking such pills.

Pan products are exported to more than 40 countries where consumers wondered how an industry that connotes home remedies and self-help could exhibit such egregious corporate mischief, if true as alleged.

Clearly, alternative medicine has acquired much legitimacy in recent memory. Otherwise, the Pan affair would not be that much of a shock: After all, quackery is quackery.

Thus frightened consumers then turned to those made in North America, but the appearance of mad cow disease in Canada in May 2003 and in the United States in December 2003 should set alarm bells off again.

Why?

Although many consumers may think of nutritional supplements as being invariably safe because they are supposedly "natural" and plant-based, most of them do contain products of animal origin, such as gelatin. Used in soft-gel capsules and dry tablets, gelatin is derived from cow bones or skin.

Then, there are what are called "glandulars", nutritional supplements containing dried and ground-up animal glands, including cow pituitary and pineal glands in the brain, which may pose an even higher risk. But it is mainly the use of cow bones that renders gelatin a Trojan horse carrying mad cow disease, properly known as bovine spongiform encephalopathy (BSE).

True, about a dozen years ago, the World Health Organisation, the United States Food and Drug Administration (FDA), and the then-European Community's Committee on BSE had, independently of one another, found that gelatin produced using methods known to reduce infectivity was safe to use.

However, in 2000, Britain's official BSE Inquiry found that farm animals were being fed possibly infected meat and bone meal. It also uncovered fresher evidence that the manufacturing processes used did not inactivate BSE as originally believed.

In particular, the use of cattle heads and, less commonly, their backbones or spinal columns, is very common. This poses a high risk because infected brain tissue may contaminate the skull — it is difficult to remove the base of the brain from the skull — while infected spinal cord tissue may contaminate the backbone. Meanwhile, British and North American farmers continue to feed herbivores such as cattle, sheep, pigs and chickens with unmarketable animal parts.

It was the feeding of cattle herds with sheep infected with scrapie, an equivalent of BSE, that led to the initial outbreak of BSE in Britain in 1985. From there, it spread to the European continent and then jumped into humans.

In infected humans, the brain develops sponge-like holes and builds up plaques. The illness lasts about 14 months and invariably ends in a horrible death.

In 1996, the British government officially admitted that BSE had jumped into humans. Yet every month that year, Britain exported 600 tonnes of gelatin to non-BSE countries for use in processed food, which was then exported to many Asian countries, say, Singapore.

The following year, the FDA acknowledged these risks and reversed its position on gelatin. In November 2000, it asked American firms manufacturing or importing dietary supplements to ensure they were BSE-free.

But compliance was, and continues to be, voluntary, with no penalties for non-compliance nor measures for monitoring compliance. This is because, believing that dietary supplements including herbs and amino acids were safe, the US Congress passed a law in 1994 to deregulate the industry so that consumers would have greater access to these products. Responding to heavy lobbying by industry, the US passed its Dietary Supplement Health and Education Act in 1994, a law that permitted makers of, say, gingko biloba or evening primrose oil to say anything about such products as long as they did not claim to cure or prevent a specific illness.

Makers were allowed to use vague language like "improves brain power" but not "prevents strokes". Also, the law required the US government, not the maker, to prove that a product was unsafe. The law specifically prevented the FDA from classifying such supplements as drugs it could regulate stringently.

Under this law, the FDA has no power to review such supplements before they hit the market and it is for the FDA to prove that a certain supplement is unsafe.

Because supplements were allowed on the market bearing non-specific but impressive claims, consumers began to see them as legitimate health products.

Thus, a mere five years after 1994, the sales of supplements had skyrocketed from US$8 billion to US$16 billion, with exports to many countries in Asia where governments responded to this influx of herbals and supplements by formulating largely similar regulation.

In Asia, no country has licensing requirements for the import, manufacture and marketing of these health supplements or of traditional remedies like jamu or Ayurvedic or Chinese preparations. In Singapore, for example, its Health Sciences Authority (HSA) only carries out post-marketing surveillance for side-effects.

Manufacturers of supplements or traditional remedies or herbal preparations such as royal jelly or echinacea, are not subject to regulation so the manufacturer has many degrees of freedom as long as it makes no specific medical claims concerning specific illnesses including diabetes, hypertension or cancer.

These products are not evaluated but, for the public, the fact that they are allowed on the market is perceived erroneously as an official stamp of approval.

This means that, in what is a very competitive business, a wayward manufacturer like Pan might sacrifice product safety and efficacy to save the bottom-line.

So there is the big business of alternative medicine on one side poised against the small man, on the other, but there is only minimalist regulation in between. The Pan episode suggests that governments everywhere might need to review that regulatory approach in a hurry. Prior to the 1994 law, however, manufacturers had to prove their products were safe before being sold in the US or exported worldwide. Unfortunately, that's no longer true. Yes, the FDA can detain shipments of high-risk materials from countries with BSE outbreaks, say, but, in practice, only 1 per cent of imports are inspected and none from non-infected nations.

In addition, inspection needs to be continued for many years after the initial outbreak, given that the disease has a long incubation period, but this is hardly done.

Unsurprisingly, many scientists and consumer groups think that the US government's preventive measures are insufficient. This claim seems less and less sensationalist today, considering that Canada and the US share the longest unmanned border in the world.

Thus Asian consumers popping health supplements imported from North America need to ask themselves: "Can you get mad cow (or some other exotic) disease from a vitamin?"

Beware of what you put in your mouth.

Coffee can be good for you

DO you fancy a cappuccino or macchiato at Starbucks now and then, or everyday of the week? There seems to be a smidgen of guilt that always goes with that cup of silky smooth mocha and it's been that way for a long time.

Originally found on shrubs in the hills of Ethiopia, shepherds noticed their sheep stayed awake all night after eating the cherries.

The bean was taken across the Red Sea to Yemen around AD1400, where people turned it into a pungent fermented beverage called qahwah. Sufi mystics would quaff copious amounts of qahwah prior to their ecstatic exercises. Before each draught, they would shout: "Ya qawi!" meaning "O strong one!", meaning their deity.

Qawi, some historians believe, is the root word for coffee. In 1542, the Ottoman empire tried unsuccessfully to ban the "sinful" drink. By the early 1600s, European coffee shops were serving it, not fermented, but as the hot beverage we now know.

When Venice imported the beans for the first time in 1615, the Catholic Church immediately denounced it as "the drink of infidels".

Caffeine is that which jump-starts some and gives others the jitters, of course. Normally, a hormone-of-sorts called adenosine slows down the firing of brain cells, so we fall asleep. Caffeine blocks adenosine, thus keeping you awake.

While health faddists demand decaffeinated coffee, coffee snobs say drinking decaf is like listening to Mozart through speakers from some hypermarket like Carrefour: However great the recording, it's Mozart without the top shimmers and bottom echoes.

Actually, caffeine is just a tasteless white powder. Any flavour loss comes from the decaffeination process itself. In the Swiss water process, raw beans are soaked in hot water until they give up their caffeine and aromatic oils.

The water is then run through charcoal filters to remove the caffeine.

That water is then recombined with the beans, which reabsorb all the aromatic stuff.

In the European process, raw beans are steamed in a rotating drum to release the caffeine, then rinsed for 12 hours with a solvent like methylene chloride to leach out the caffeine.

Little solvent is left behind — methylene chloride evaporates at 40 deg C whereas coffee is roasted at 205 deg C, so any solvent should burn off.

"Thus, there is no detectable methylene chloride in a cup of Starbucks decaf coffee", says the gourmet coffee leader, which uses the chemical except with its decaf Mocca Java, which is produced via the water process.

Yet, concerns remain.

The United States banned the use of methylene chloride in hairsprays after laboratory mice developed cancers with it. Workers handling it at decaffeination plants are told to handle it with extreme caution. A safer alternative is ethyl acetate, a compound found in apples, pears and peaches but some people develop a skin reaction to it. On balance, the water process seems best — or just drink non-decaffeinated.

The US National Cancer Institute says most of the 20,000 studies carried out worldwide have not found a link between coffee and cancer. In fact, coffee may lower the risk of colon cancer, liver cirrhosis, gallstones, Parkinson's disease and asthma.

Still, six cups a day could increase the artery-clogging cholesterol and triglyceride in your blood. Two coffee oils called cafestol and kahweol that are released when you add hot water to coffee grounds cause those increases. But a paper filter used in the drip method traps the oils.

In Europe, coffee is often boiled with water and sieved. The fine metal mesh in those chic plunger-style or French-press coffee-makers cannot filter the two culprits out. Gold-plated filters like those you can get as a mug-set at Starbucks don't remove them either.

Finally, the espresso method of passing very hot steam through coffee grounds, including espresso, cappuccino and cafe latte, is no better. You need paper which, the aficionado says, adds an unwelcome taste to the brew. For the rest of us, though, a few daily cups of paper-filtered non-decaf Java may do us some good.

You can't go wrong with instant too. Instant coffee is brewed in huge vats and only water-soluble parts are used in its manufacture so the two harmful oils are left behind.

But then instant is for heathens.

Should you stick with non-stick Teflon pans?

FROM frying pans to muffin trays, the cookware and bakeware in many a home today are likely to be non-stick. None of these utensils carries warning labels.

But perhaps they should.

It appears that non-stick Teflon coat may be a sticky problem, that non-stick can make you sick. Teflon, the most slippery substance on earth, keeps eggs from sticking to pans or bacon from burning, and makes pots easier to wash. If the coating gets hot enough, the fumes it gives off have been known to kill birds. In these cases of Teflon-toxicosis, as they are called, the bird's lungs bleed and fill up with fluid, so the animal drowns in its own secretions.

If birds keel over and die from Teflon fumes, what about the cook?

First, the fumes can give humans a flu-like illness.

Teflon manufacturer DuPont, the second biggest chemical-maker in the United States, acknowledges that the fumes — you won't smell or see any smoke — can cause a condition in humans called "polymer fume fever". This is a short, flu-like illness lasting up to two days, with headaches, backaches, chills, and a temperature between 37.7 and 40 deg C.

DuPont admits it is unsafe to use Teflon-coated cookware at temperatures above 260 deg C — although significant breakdown does not occur until 340 deg C, which it claims is well above normal cooking temperatures.

Thus, the company argues, in day-to-day kitchen use, Teflon-coated pots and pans don't get hot enough to release those fumes.

Yet, tests have shown that after only two minutes on the stove, a Teflon-coated pan hits 260 deg C — at which point bacon only begins to get crispy, so it isn't quite done yet. At 290 deg C, ultra-fine particles start coming off the Teflon coating. The hotter it gets, the more these are released, increasing the risk of them being inhaled deep into the lungs. Teflon-coated cookware can even reach 370 deg C in three to five minutes, when the coatings release 15 harmful gases and chemicals, including two carcinogens and a chemical warfare agent used in the two world wars.

In fact, toxic particles that can kill birds are produced at even lower temperatures. For example, in a peer-reviewed experiment conducted in

1998 by University of Missouri scientists, 2,400 chicks were placed in pens warmed by heat lamp bulbs coated with Teflon that were operating at only 202 deg C. Within three days, with all other causes of death excluded, 52 per cent of the birds were dead.

By now, you should be wondering if that's all.

Could other hazards lurk in Teflon?

Possibly.

After decades of denial, DuPont was charged in July 2004 by the US government with illegally withholding evidence between 1981 and 2001 that a chemical called perfluorooctanoic acid, or C8 — a waxy, soap-like compound used to make Teflon — poses "substantial risk of injury to human health".

If proven, this could cost DuPont big bucks. The company denies the charges, but C8 has been shown to cause liver damage and reproductive problems in rats. Higher risks of birth defects and developmental problems in pregnancies of exposed women have also been observed. C8 can be absorbed by people working in Teflon plants or simply from the environment. Entirely man-made, it is semi-volatile and can be spread by the wind: It has turned up in the blood of people and animals in areas far removed from where Teflon is made or used, including remote areas of China. In one large US sample of thousands, 90 per cent tested positive for C8 in their blood, especially children.

Consumers should care because we don't yet know how C8 actually finds its way into our blood. Scientists are now scrambling to establish this, because the answer will tell us if we can absorb the substance from everyday items with Teflon coatings.

The possibility that Teflon used to protect carpets and upholstery may give off the chemical cannot be ruled out. It could also be absorbed directly through the skin from stainproof apparel coated with Teflon. Or some nail polish.

Then, there is grease-resistant food packaging used by fast-food restaurants, like French fries cartons and pizza boxes, as well as paper plates and microwave popcorn bags. Often, a very small Teflon-like polymer is used to keep grease from seeping through paper or cardboard. When ingested, the compound can break down into C8 within our bodies. So people could be ingesting C8 transferred from packaging to food. Although this has not been ascertained, studies show that at least one similar compound used in paper-protection applications is readily found in the blood of those exposed to it.

More generally, the greatest worry is possible long-term effects in a generation that has grown up using Teflon products, including fast-food packaging. Tracking C8 has not been done heretofore because it is an unregulated chemical, so users don't have to report it to the authorities. The US government began its own inquiries in April 2003 and, pending its results, says consumers need not stop using Teflon products.

So what to do until the verdict is in? You could limit the use of Teflon-coated things, especially cookware. If you keep using such cookware, put food into your non-stick pan quickly so it doesn't get too hot too soon.

Also, cook at lower rather than higher temperatures.

Or, you could just switch to stainless steel cookware and aluminum bakeware. Yes, food might stick but there won't be any toxic fumes — and perhaps your kitchen canary will get to live a little longer.

Microwave ovens are safe, just keep the eggs away

IMAGINE being nearly blinded by flying shards of eggshell. It did happen to a nine-year-old girl who was cradling a microwaved egg when it exploded in her face, the *British Medical Journal* (BMJ) reported in early 2004. Surgery has since restored her eyesight.

Though the microwave oven has been widely used since the late 1980s, urban legends about microwave accidents still abound. Then, there is always that friend who has pulled the plug on the oven altogether for fear of cancer.

So is it safe to use?

The answer hinges on how the oven actually works. When it is turned on, an electron tube called the magnetron begins to emit microwaves, which bounce around inside the oven from wall to wall — like beams of light in a room of mirrors — until they are absorbed by food or dissipated in the air.

However, each microwave has so little energy that it can't directly break chemical bonds inside food to cause rearrangements in a molecule. Thus, no chemical changes occur, which is why food cooked in the microwave oven is generally quite bland.

Rather than inducing chemical changes, microwaves cause only physical changes. How? Store-bought microwave ovens produce waves that are 2.45 GHz in frequency, which means they change direction 2.45 billion times a second. Like all other radio or electromagnetic waves, microwaves consist of electric force fields. This means that, when the magnetron is turned on, an electric field is fluctuating back and forth inside the chamber 2.45 billion times a second.

Any electrically charged particle inside the chamber is sitting in the midst of such a field, so it gets pulled back and forth 2.45 billion times a second. Now, each water molecule has two negatively charged oxygen atoms at one end and a positively charged hydrogen atom at the other. Because opposites attract, each hydrogen of a water molecule inside food is attracted to all other oxygen atoms around it.

Standing amid the oven's electric field, these water molecules are twisted back and forth at a red-hot pace, so some hydrogen is always being pulled away from the oxygens. While the attractive forces between the hydrogens and oxygens are tiny, a lot of them can add up to a sizeable force.

When such water molecules that are attracted to one another are twisted and rubbed against one another billions of times per second, friction heats things up. The heat then cooks food the usual way, denaturising protein as in hardening egg whites, for example, or caramelising sugar so it becomes dark brown.

Is this any different from industrialists zapping their rice, potatoes or beef with radioactive rays to extend their shelf life?

By a mile. Something like uranium produces radioactive waves that change their directions millions of trillions of times a second. At these frequencies, they have so much more energy than microwaves that they can even penetrate concrete walls and actually change (ionise) the molecular structure of matter. For instance, they can change DNA molecules in our cells, causing genetic mutations.

Here's the crux of the matter: Intensity is all-important with any kind of radiation. Because microwaves have so little energy, they can't change any molecular structure. That's why they are called "non-ionising" waves. The only way microwaves can harm you is if they cook you. Say, you decide to operate the oven with the door ajar, then stick a finger inside. That will hurt.

(By the way, mobile phones also emit microwaves next to your ear — they work by sending also 2.45 GHz microwave signals to the nearest receiving tower — so some minor cooking may be occurring at your ear. But their wattage or power is so small that the cooking won't affect you and, as microwaves are non-ionising, the cancer risk is probably nil.)

Still, you are concerned that microwaves might leak from the oven?

Well, they won't — if the door seal is well made.

Yes, the cooking chamber has mesh-covered holes to let hot air out but these holes are smaller than microwaves — which are actually 12.2 cm long each — so they can't pass through. Because metal reflects microwaves, they bounce right back in as if there were no holes, so there is no leakage there.

Even the mesh you see on the glass door acts as a metal shield — the holes are also under 12.2 cm — so microwaves also get reflected back in. Despite these holes then, the whole chamber acts as if it were a solid metal box keeping microwaves in.

What if the seal is faulty, though?

In that case, leakage does occur. But just keep a meter away from the oven: Very little of any radiation is left at that distance. This is because microwaves disperse and dissipate very quickly in the air, exactly like feeling the warmth when your hand is very near a flame but not feeling it a metre away.

So is it safe enough for children to operate microwave ovens unsupervised?

Well, not quite. There is one big danger: Cooking eggs. Under some circumstances, microwaved water inside an egg can become hotter than the 100 deg C reached in ordinary boiling. As water inside the egg white begins to vaporise, it begins to build up pressure until it's enough to break the shell, causing a sudden explosion at that point. With a particularly hard shell, the egg can be a time bomb, as the nine-year-old in the BMJ report discovered.

So don't wait for manufacturers to plaster a prominent warning against heating eggs in the oven.

Just tell your children today.

Index